Live
Learn
Grow

Lessons of a Reluctant Tiger

Brannon Beliso

Copyright © 2017 Brannon Beliso

ISBN: 978-1-63492-086-5

All rights reserved. No part of this publication may be reproduced, stored in a retrieval system, or transmitted in any form or by any means, electronic, mechanical, recording or otherwise, without the prior written permission of the author.

Published by BookLocker.com, Inc., St. Petersburg, Florida.

Printed on acid-free paper.

BookLocker.com, Inc.
2017

First Edition

"If I am living
Then I am learning.
And if I am learning,
Then I am growing."
—Brannon Beliso

DEDICATION

I dedicate this book to my sister Lisa and my mama, Barbara, and to all those who were gone way too soon.

I pray your faces are the first I see when God calls me home.

GRATITUDE

I truly believe that we do not do this thing called "life" alone and isn't that a beautiful thing? Just to be able to offer my gratitude to all of you here has made writing this book all that more humbling.

To my wife, Kim, I have loved you forever. You are living proof that angels really do exist.

To my children, Brannon, Brayden and Teya, you are my heart and purpose.

To my sister Lorraine, thanks for always having my back since the days of 15th Street.

To my papa, I wish life could have been different for us. I still have so much to learn from you.

To Magic, your unconditional friendship is a gift that needs no words.

To my family, friends and believers, you inspire me to keep giving and making a difference.

To John Cocoran, my writing mentor, your tutelage has given me a voice to create with words.

To Rick Alemany, my martial arts instructor, who has always been like a dad to me, thank you for being the only person to ever say to me, "I am proud of you, Son."

To the team at One Martial Arts, it is because of your dedication and support that I have the freedom to spend more life with my family and pursue my creative purpose.

To the many others who are too numerous to name here, I am a better person because of the experiences we have shared and the valuable lessons I have learned.

Contents

DEAR GOD

I am humbled to be an instrument of Your will.

I thank You for the creativity You bless me with to truly make a difference.

I pray that You will allow me to serve others by being an example to inspire them to live their best lives.

May everyone with whom I am blessed to share life know that You love us more than we could possibly comprehend.

Grant me the wisdom to accept life on life's terms; the strength to affect change where needed; and the humility to let go of people and things that do not challenge me to be my best.

May I continue to learn and grow through my mistakes but have the clarity to not make the same mistakes over and over.

And through my purpose of service and faith, may I witness Your true love and mercy.

INVITATION

Humbly, I invite you to live your best life through learning, growing and cultivating a mindset that is rich in positive and empowering life skills—skills such as focus, discipline, confidence, integrity and commitment.

I am passionate about mastering the way I think because I know from firsthand experience what it means to be a prisoner of my own negative thinking. Greed, selfishness, self-loathing and lust were debilitating and counter-productive, and they prevented me from living my best life.

It was my choice to live and act from a negative mindset. But leaving bad habits behind was difficult for me because, as a child, I felt helpless and at the mercy of poverty and the abusive adults in my life. I felt powerless during most of my childhood. At the age of 11 months, I was placed in foster care, which lasted for three years. I was molested at the ages of 8 and 12. This feeling of powerlessness carried into my adulthood and led me to make some bad choices. I saw myself as a product of my upbringing—a victim—so I lived my life as one.

For many years of my adult life, I walked around in pain, like a wounded child trying to relive my past and change it. My inability to accept life on life's terms was preventing me from living each day to the fullest.

Now I know I cannot change my past. But I can choose to look at it as some of life's greatest lessons to help me live my best life today. I accept that my past helped shape me, but it does not define who I am today; the choices I make and the actions I take are what do that.

Gratefully, I recognize I can learn new life skills and habits that help me create a life worth living. We all want the best of life, but to deserve the best, you have to do and be your best. It requires us to be willing to take ownership of the choices we make to learn, grow and live a different life today.

In this book, I share experiences that have greatly impacted my life. I take the lessons that I have learned to create a life of service and purpose. You can read it from cover to cover, or simply open it at random. However you choose to do it, read it with the courage, faith and hope to live, learn and grow.

THE NET OVER MY CRIB

When I told my sister Lisa that I saw a white grid whenever I closed my eyes to go to sleep, she looked at me with a deep sense of sadness and asked, "You don't know what that is, do you?"

I shrugged my shoulders and offered her a half-hearted "No."

Lisa confessed, "That was the net they put over your crib in YGC so you couldn't climb out."

YGC, or the *Youth Guidance Center*, was the first stop in the California foster care system, a system that my sister and I were part for about three years. My parents' stories have never matched up, but I believe Lisa was about 3 years old and I was 11 months when we first went in. What I do know is that my father had taken off to Los Angeles to get away from my mother, who drank heavily. She left us with the next-door neighbor for the evening so she could go out and party. That party turned into a five-day drinking binge.

Sometime during those five days, I became sick with croup and had to be taken to St. Luke Hospital's emergency room. My windpipe was swelling shut, and the doctor considered a tracheotomy to help me breathe. The hospital staff asked where my parents were. When the neighbor told them my parents had taken off days ago, it triggered a call to Child Protective Services, and we became part of the system. The only saving grace of this moment was that I responded to the breathing treatments and they did not have to cut a hole in my throat and insert a tube so I could breathe.

During the next three years, my parents were given supervised visitation and, eventually, unsupervised visitation, until they could prove they were fit parents, and we could return to their custody.

I can remember those Sunday visits when my parents picked us up at Mrs. Valencia's, our designated caregiver. Mrs. Valencia had three boys of her own, and they constantly bullied my sister and me. They were all older than we were, but Lisa and I never backed down from their attacks. I still carry a scar on the side of my head from when one of the boys pushed me off the back stairs, and I hit my head on a brick.

During visitations, my parents often took us to Playland, an amusement and carnival attraction at Ocean Beach in San Francisco. Playland is long gone but Laughing Sal, the automated character who graced the front of the Fun House, still holds court in a museum at Fisherman's Wharf. I have visited her from time to time when we are doing the tourist thing with relatives or friends from out of town. When I do, I find myself reliving those three years with a deep sense of reflection.

One of the hard life lessons I learned from my time in foster care was how a traumatic life experience, especially at a young age, can have such a big impact.

It wasn't until my late twenties that I really understood how much of my past was negatively impacting my present. If I continued to live in the past, I would never be happy. I had to stop blaming my parents for the life I was living. Even though I was physically an adult, I behaved like a wounded child. I justified the poor decisions I made because of my dysfunctional upbringing. I recognized that I needed to *change.* I truly wanted to, and clearly understood that nothing would change until I changed it. I needed to stop being a victim and take complete ownership of who I was and the choices I made in life.

Once I knew I had to change, doors opened, allowing me to act on that knowledge and begin that change. As Confucius said, "A journey of a thousand miles begins with a single step." By taking action incrementally, using healthy and balanced life skills, we learn the core values that move us toward our goals. I wanted to know how to balance my mind, body and spirit, so I read everything I could get my hands on regarding self-help. I attended lectures and workshops. I participated in different churches and learned spiritual practices. I continued to live life on life's terms, but with a purpose to learn and grow into my *truer self*, the person I was intended to be.

REPORT CARD

I was very proud of my report card. I had straight A's! I was 10 years old and couldn't wait to show my father, hoping to earn his approval. I handed my report card to him. He gave it the once over and cleared his throat, just as he always did when he was about to make a point.

"What is this A-minus?" my father asked in a tone of disappointment. Honestly, I hadn't even noticed it. I didn't have an answer for him but felt like my best would never be good enough, so why even try.

This defeatist thinking owned me for the better part of my twenties. I moved from one broken relationship to another, and from starting one mediocre business to another, none ever quite reaching the level of success I knew it could.

Several years of therapy and countless self-help groups brought me to the realization that you cannot live your life simply to please another. In every experience where you live for that approval, you move further away from your truer self.

I always felt a sense of resignation with each failed attempt to gain my father's praise. I knew at a heart level that trying to do so would never get me the results I desired. I hid behind the rationalization that, when I fell short, at least I could say, "I tried!"

One night, I found myself sitting in a movie theater watching *Return of the Jedi*. In the scene where Yoda instructs Luke Skywalker to use the Force to lift his X-Wing Fighter out of a bog, Luke halfheartedly says to Yoda, "All right, I'll give it a try." Yoda responds with the Zen-like philosophy, "Do or do not. There is no try." It hit me! Either I was going to do this thing called "life" without making excuses and blaming others, or I was going to "try" my way into a life that was never mine. Then and there, I decided I would no longer be a people-pleaser who put my values and purpose second to validation from others.

I walked out of the theater that night with a clear purpose. Nike's "Just Do It" slogan made sense now. I was determined to create a life worthy of the stories I'm sharing with you here. In my mind, I held that report card with straight A's again, filled with pride reserved for me and no one else.

FOOD STAMPS, DENTED CANS AND PURPLE SNEAKERS

For a time during my childhood, my family was on welfare and food stamps. My father had a lot of pride, so when it was time to go grocery shopping, he always sent my sisters and me. We shopped at The Dented Can Store, which sold discounted cans of food. The meat was always suspect, having a weird brown hue to it, with several expiration date labels strategically placed over the previous ones. I would peel the labels back to find the most accurate date, making sure we didn't buy bad meat. Most of the time, though, I just gave up and bought bologna, Vienna sausage or Spam. I found it cool that the bologna bubbled up like a dome when I fried it. And when I cooked Spam, I swore it tasted like steak.

What I hated most about grocery shopping was when I had to present the food stamps at the checkout counter. Embarrassed, I'd look down at the floor as I handed them to the clerk. It felt as if everyone in the store was looking right at me. I laugh about it now because, in hindsight, most of the people in that line were probably using food stamps, too.

Because we couldn't afford to buy new clothes, we shopped at Goodwill and the Purple Heart thrift stores. It was common in our household to recycle clothing several times, passing them down from the biggest to the smallest of the four kids. I, being the only boy, would often get my father's hand-me-downs, and I even recall wearing one of his suits to my high school graduation.

A memory from my childhood that shaped one of my strongest core values was the day my younger sister, Lorraine, chose to wear my purple Converse High Tops to school. As I mentioned, hand-me-downs were common in our house, but this was different. Even though my shoes were at least three sizes too big for her, she insisted on wearing them because it was picture day. I remember thinking, as she marched down the street to school, that her shoes didn't matter because they won't photograph her feet. I didn't say anything because she was on a mission, inspired by the fact that she could fill her brother's shoes. Lorraine walked as if she was 10 feet tall! I understood her desire to wear my shoes had nothing to do with picture day, but was because she looked up to me and was proud to be my sister.

The experience of that day stayed with me. Witnessing my sister's purpose, the impact and potential we have to influence another was so relevant. Regardless if I wanted to accept responsibility, I understood I was the best example for her to follow at the time. A deep sense of humility came over me, and I was inspired to want to be better than I ever thought I could be.

Secondly, I've never feared disappointing my sister because I know she loves me to the moon and back. Without that fear to hinder me, I have always been able to be my best, even when I was at my worst. To have someone love us unconditionally is one of the greatest gifts life can offer. It is also one of the greatest assets because that unconditional love inspires us to achieve our goals and dreams, and never give up. So, if you have people like this in your corner (and I believe we all do), value them with all of your heart. Express your gratitude to them every chance you get, and know that you are truly blessed.

I am humbled by the influence my sister and I have had on one another. To this day, our relationship is one of my greatest motivators to live my life by being the best example for others to follow.

TOURNAMENT

Again around 10 years old, I was competing in The Internationals, one of the biggest martial arts tournaments in the world, and I was in contention for first place. My father, an accomplished martial artist himself, was my instructor and coach. He had a strategy to beat my opponent and his instructions to me were very clear. But once I got into the ring, things didn't work out as planned, and I needed to make some adjustments to win. I was so excited to hear my name announced over the loudspeaker! The tournament promoter, Ed Parker, handed me my trophy in front of close to 10,000 people. I ran off the stage to celebrate with my father but, as I approached him, he was wearing that same look of disappointment he had worn when he saw that A-minus on my report card...with one difference. He was clenching his jaw, which meant he was *angry*.

"Why didn't you follow my instructions and do what I told you to do?" he shouted for all to hear. Again, I had no answer for him. "Get down now and do pushups until I tell you to stop!" he shouted even louder, as he snatched the trophy out of my hands. My father stood over me menacingly as I did those pushups. I was embarrassed by his reaction, but it taught me a valuable life lesson.

I learned that being an individual, expressing my creativity, and making my own choices based on my personal vision and intuition, were going to leave some people unhappy. At that moment, I understood the saying, "If you're going to make an omelet, you are going to have to break a few eggs."

This experience only fueled the conviction to live to my full potential. No longer would I make excuses or fall in line like a sheep being led to slaughter. It strengthened my purpose and passion to live my best life without limitations.

After the tournament, there was no turning back. While this conviction cost me my relationship with my father, I would have paid an even greater price if I had lost myself (as I had so many times before). Choosing to gain acceptance from my father (and others) over being true to myself has always yielded negative results. And as I continue to learn, I see that it is possible to be true to yourself while offering others unconditional love. My childlike heart and wishful thinking will always long for this with my father, but I humbly accept that has never been the case.

The greatest gift my father offered me was the lesson that I cannot control other people. I saw this in my relationship with him every day. My father disapproved of me when I thought for myself and did not do what he thought I should. To him, this was unacceptable.

On the flipside, my father taught me acceptance of and tolerance toward others. The reality of these events with him made me realize I am not in control of circumstances and other people. It has shown me how to be more accountable for my thoughts, choices and actions, and for the way I choose to live my life each day. My relationship with my dad is a constant reminder that whenever I am pointing my finger at someone, there are three pointing back at me. I must take responsibility for the fingers pointing back without making excuses or blaming others for my life.

The journey and path to enlightenment are inward. There is nothing anyone can give me that I can't give myself. Every answer I seek is truly within. It has often been my choice to reach for external devices for fulfillment. There is that common belief that more money, a new car, bigger home, different job or relationship, will make us happy. We often chase these things only to find ourselves still unfulfilled and discontented.

The good news is that we all have the ability to change whatever we don't like about ourselves. But beware, this journey feels lonely at times. Such growth requires willingness to pull back our covers and take an honest look at ourselves. Even when we don't like what we see, this simple act of acceptance is a great place to begin. Only through this honest and rigorous self-assessment can we begin to walk a path toward the person we desire and aspire to be.

A BIG PIECE OF CARDBOARD

In 1950, my dad came to America from the Philippines on a boat. He was 15 years old, had a sixth-grade education, and $15 in his pocket. The U.S. Immigration Department detained him for six months before releasing him onto Market Street in San Francisco. His first jobs were working in a factory taking pleats out of skirts, and at a racetrack as a stable boy tending to the horses. He stayed in an immigrant family's flat, sleeping on a folding cot in the kitchen. Each day, he rose before everyone else; the family needed the kitchen to make breakfast.

My dad said that the level of racism at that time was not exclusive. The prejudice was aimed at all ethnicities not well-off and white. He was determined to make something of himself, but knew it would not be easy.

I remember this story of my dad's life because he said something that made a profound impact on my life: "At that time, others were smarter than me, richer than me, and whiter than me. But the one thing I knew I had over all of them was that I was willing to work harder than any of them."

My dad instilled this work ethic in me throughout my youth. We were always working on some project together. Whether it was remodeling a bathroom or sheetrocking a wall, we worked hard. My dad's form of punishment was to make my sisters and me do chores. He was determined to teach us to work harder than others, so we understood the value of having a great work ethic.

One day, my dad told me we needed to change the brake shoes on our car. Being from a poor family meant we never took the car to the auto repair shop for any kind of repair. For that matter, we never even went to the doctor unless it was an absolute emergency.

I was bit concerned and wondered what my dad was thinking. He had never changed the brakes on any car, let alone the one that we had to drive around in safely. Back then, you could not simply "Google it" or watch a DIY video to learn how to undertake such a task.

I followed him out to the curb, curious as to how my dad was going to accomplish this chore. Walking slightly behind him, I noticed he was carrying a big piece of cardboard along with some tools, a roll of silver duct tape and a black marker.

My dad proceeded to jack up the front end of our car and remove both front tires. He laid the cardboard down on the sidewalk closest to the left front brake assembly, which was now exposed. He then began to take it apart, piece by piece. As he did, he taped each piece of the brake assembly to the cardboard and numbered it with the black marker in the order it was removed. By the time he stripped it down and reassembled it on the cardboard with duct tape, he had a perfect replica of the left brake assembly.

He then proceeded to replace the worn-out brake shoes with new ones. Then, methodically, using his ingenious self-made instructions (pre-IKEA), he put the brake back together, exactly as if it had never been touched. He periodically referenced the exposed right wheel brake as a way of double-checking what he was doing. After my father completed the left front brake, he repeated the process on the right.

The great life lesson I learned from this mechanical adventure with my dad was the value of being resourceful and figuring things out for myself. A benefit of being poor was that, by default, your only choice was that you had to do it yourself.

This thinking has been powerful in helping me create a life that is all my own. I blame no one for my life because I am the one making it. I have my own big piece of cardboard and I am writing the instructions for my life.

This *Do It Yourself* mindset built my self-confidence and continues to do so today. It allows me to make mistakes on the path of self-discovery. I'm convinced that no mistake is a mistake unless I squander the opportunity to learn and grow from it. I am too busy figuring it out to have time to climb upon a pity pot of "poor me" and self-entitlement.

The bottom line is that this is my space and my race, and I'm the only person who can live it. To be happy and successful, it requires me to be a thinker who learns the rules, then breaks them to create my own. It challenges me to think outside the box and, better yet, forget the box entirely and think for myself.

MAGIC BOY

I used to be a singer and recording artist in the Philippines. One day, as I was on my way to do a TV show to promote my album, I found myself stuck in some crazy traffic. I ranted and raved to my driver about the traffic jam, like some spoiled, entitled wannabe rock star, when I was blessed with one of those "aha" moments.

I looked over to the side of the road and saw a young boy playing with a stick and a rock. By the dirty clothes he wore and the cardboard shack behind him, it was obvious he was living in extreme poverty. But this kid, surrounded by poverty, chaos, traffic, pollution and hordes of people, was *happy.* His smile radiated around him as he moved in graceful symmetry with his stick and rock. It felt surreal. The light of his smile was a huge contradiction to what I perceived as a sad situation. Time stood still.

The magic of watching this boy's pure joy only gave way to the embarrassment I suddenly felt for my own self-absorbed behavior. It was as if someone had kicked me hard in the stomach. I sunk down in the back seat of the car, hoping that no one would see me. Here I was with what I thought was the end-all, be-all music career. I was supposed to be happy, right? But compared to this kid, I felt like I had nothing. In a moment, he taught me that happiness is a choice, independent of our circumstances; it is a state of mind each of us chooses.

I woke up and understood that the trappings of my so-called fame and material possessions were not true happiness.

This boy changed my life forever. Shortly after this experience, I gave up my music career and life in the Philippines, and headed back to the U.S. to find and fulfill my true purpose. It's true...the richest person is the one who can be happiest with the least.

LIVING MY LIFE WITHOUT YOU

On December 14, 2001, I received a call from my brother-in-law, as I was about to teach a kickboxing class at my martial arts school in San Francisco. Sobbing heavily, he told me that my eldest sister, Lisa, had just passed away, and I needed to come home immediately. Somehow, I made it to my car. Driving down the highway in the pouring winter rain, I could hear myself begging, "Please Lord, please Lord, please Lord." I was in the middle of this bad dream and I was wide-awake.

As I arrived home, I expected to find an ambulance or a fire truck in front of the house. But, to my confusion, it seemed like any other day with only my sister's car parked in the driveway. With a false sense of relief, I ran into the house half-expecting to see Lisa sitting at the kitchen table, putting on her makeup, as usual. As I came through the front door, I saw my cousin Sharisse sitting on the couch. It was painfully obvious that she had been crying. The truth in her eyes destroyed any hope that this was all a bad dream. When I asked Sharisse where Lisa was, she pointed to my bedroom door. My heart ached. My sister liked to come into my room to connect with me after a busy day, or to say goodnight. At other times, when I wasn't home, she found solace in the empty bed in my room...a welcome relief from the crowded one she shared with her husband and my two nephews.

With each step toward my bedroom, I felt the weight of sadness grow. I opened the door. Lisa was lying on the floor, in her favorite flowered flannel pajamas, rollers still in her hair. I struggled to take it all in. I heard the words come out of my mouth from a place far away, "We can't leave her like this." Strangely enough, my concern at that moment was that Lisa would never want anyone to see her with her hair in rollers. I proceeded to take them out, put a pillow under her head, and cover her with a blanket. With tears falling from my eyes, I wrapped my arms around her and held her, not wanting to let her go.

At some point, my cousin came into the room. She knelt to comfort me as I held Lisa. We found ourselves reciting the Lord's Prayer. As we did, I swear I could feel my sister's soul leave her body, passing upward, directly through my chest and out my back. It was a warm, peaceful energy moving through me. At that moment, I was awakened to the truth that our lives do not end here, and that we do pass on to something else. I couldn't prove what that something was but it was *real*. I had just witnessed the true meaning of faith—an unwavering belief in something that can't be seen or physically proven.

I learned later that the ambulance and fire department had already come and gone before me. Lisa died in my bed and they had moved her to the floor to try to revive her. The coroner's vehicle had broken down on the way to the house, which is why Lisa was still there. I believe that God intended for it to happen as it did, because Lisa needed to wait for me to say goodbye. As I held her, she still felt warm...as if she were sleeping. As I felt her spirit pass through me, I knew I would never see her again in this lifetime, and that she was gone.

Several days later, I found myself standing in church, delivering my sister's eulogy in front of 400 grieving people. As I looked out at them, I said, "This is both the saddest and happiest day of my life." I could see their confusion and even shock at my comment. "I would not be this sad unless I loved Lisa so completely," I continued. With Lisa's passing, I learned that the greatest gift of all is to be able to love someone with all my being. I also came to accept that love comes with great sacrifice but is worth everything.

Not only had I lost my sister, I had lost my best friend, surrogate mother and protector. From my first breath of life, Lisa was the one constant who made me feel that everything was going to be all right. Some days later, with tears in my eyes and a heavy heart, I remember writing to her in my journal, "Living my life without you is like breathing without air."

So why do I believe that sharing my sister's passing can help us all live our best life? Because life's often tragic and challenging experiences can offer us some of the greatest gifts for learning and growth— like a devastating forest fire that's needed to release seeds for new growth. We can choose to embrace these sad experiences with a humble heart, and overcome them to create an amazing life. Or...we can choose to be a victim, and allow our tragedies to imprison and have power over us.

Since Lisa's passing, I have learned never to take anything or anyone for granted. I deeply appreciate every second of life and every single breath I am blessed with. I wake up to the miracle of each new day with a deep sense of gratitude. I practice forgiveness and acceptance and I am committed to never holding on to resentments.

I celebrate Lisa's memory by living to my full potential. I believe that she would want me to miss her, but that she wouldn't want me to be sad in any way that compromises my happiness. Her passing taught me that, even at its worst, life is a precious gift. I should never squander my days by living in the pain of the past. Every day should be celebrated in the present—our one true gift.

Above all, I embrace that it takes great courage to be vulnerable and love unconditionally. I celebrate my love for Lisa by living a purpose-driven life, with a passion for service. I stand with an open heart to everything life offers, good and bad. And, I choose to do so with big love!

Living my life without you
is like breathing without air.

Living my life without you
often leaves me so sad and scared.

Still, I give a little gratitude and
thanks be to the Lord.

I made it through another day
broken heart and all.

MISTAKE OR OPPORTUNITY?

Life is often a series of missed opportunities. Every day, people walk around with their eyes wide open, but are totally asleep. These missed opportunities are lessons waiting to be learned, disguised as mistakes. These lessons challenge us to pull back our covers and take an honest look. They also present us with the opportunity to learn and become better people. The challenge is to recognize these opportunities in that moment, and learn from them…to see the potential of each mistake as an opportunity.

For me, these missed opportunities presented themselves through my countless broken relationships with women. I can honestly say that, for most of my adult life, I had never had a successful monogamous relationship. I was that guy who would never commit to a woman because I was too busy pursuing my dreams and had no time for that nonsense. I always had a million excuses as to why the relationship could not work. Or, at worst, I would lie and commit halfway to a relationship I wasn't *in* to begin with. I walked around with my eyes wide open and, yet, I was totally asleep.

I hurt a lot of people with my selfish, toxic behavior. While I know people are responsible for their own lives, I believe I was influential in one woman becoming anorexic, another ending up in therapy, and so many others exiting my life in a hail of tears. I took no prisoners in my state of sleepwalking through life.

Then I started dating a woman who had a one-year-old son named Alex. I met her about the time my sister Lisa passed away. Again, I did not have the tools to give this woman the commitment she deserved. What I didn't figure into the mix was this little boy, whose father was not in the picture.

One day I was watching Alex while his mom was working. We went to the beach to hang out and play. I held his little hand in mine as we walked down the shore. As I looked down at Alex, I woke from my self-imposed sleep. I saw an incredible opportunity, and I was not going to make a mistake and miss it.

With my sister Lisa's recent passing, I was broken and empty. People kept telling me that "time heals all" and that didn't cut it for me. Now here was Alex, a little boy who needed a father. At the time, I was not in the position to love myself. But loving this child was as natural as the waves that tickled our bare feet as we walked along the beach.

Against everyone's advice, I became Alex's dad. People close to me told me that if things did not work out with his mom (which was inevitable, given my track record), she would take him away.

Well, one year later, Alex's mom and I broke up, but she allowed me to continue to father Alex. We were like a good divorced couple. I had him weekends, summers, and most holidays. I was the father I had never known. I took every opportunity to teach, love and give my life to this boy.

Then, as everyone predicted, one weekend I called her to arrange a time to pick up Alex, and she said I could no longer see him. After almost five years of being his dad, he was gone.

I was both awake and in the middle of a nightmare. I desperately wanted to go back to sleep, so I could wake up from this bad dream. However, I got no such reprieve, and struggled to accept that Alex was really gone. For a few weeks, I tried calling him repeatedly, hoping his mom would change her mind. One day, I called and Alex answered the phone. In a voice filled with fear, he abruptly said, "I can't talk to you, Dad. I don't want to get in trouble." It was over. I had to let go, for Alex's best interest.

The lesson I learned from this amazing life experience is that to love completely and unconditionally is an opportunity none of us should miss. Despite the fear that Alex's mom might take him away, my time with Alex was the most awake I had been since my sister's death. He gave me a purpose beyond myself.

What everyone else saw as a mistake, I embraced as an opportunity to learn, live and grow. I have not seen or spoken to Alex since, but will always choose to go through life with my eyes wide open and be totally awake.

UNAUTHORIZED THOUGHT PATTERNS

I have many war stories I could tell about times I have behaved inappropriately or made bad choices. But I don't believe that is what is important to share here. I do know that whenever I was confronted about my actions and asked why I did what I did, my response was most likely, "I don't know." I honestly did not know why I chose to do some of the wrong things I did. It was as if someone else was acting through me. There was no rhyme or reason for my behavior. What I find of greater value than the insane details of my past are the lessons I have learned. I came to recognize a pattern of behavior that was debilitating and damaging to my self-esteem. I was always ashamed of my choices. Even if no one found out what I had done, I knew. The scarier part is that, at times, I could rationalize my behavior. I felt I was justified in my actions. I believed my own lies and twisted them into a warped truth. I even remember I use to say, "I'm so bad that I'm good." I romanticized my sick decisions as some cool thing. Deep down, I was a wounded child who knew it was wrong, but did it anyway. I believe this self-inflicted cycle of pain was a warning from the man I was born to be, who was crying out, "Stop it!"

I can't say I had a moment of clarity that helped me start the changes toward a better me. I like to think of myself as a work in progress. I constantly remind myself it is about *progress*, not perfection. This enabled me to keep chipping away at the things I don't like about myself, and not throw in the towel when I falter from my path.

So, by the grace of God and through the process of self-discovery, which has involved endless hours of reading, workshops, therapy and meditation, I can attribute many of my darker moments in life to what I have learned to identify as *unauthorized thought patterns*. This ill-fated mindset—*unauthorized thought patterns*—thrives on my negative experiences and influences since childhood. For example, the abuse I suffered from my parents and the time spent in foster homes left emotional scars that shaped my thinking as a child. It became the foundation of my decision-making process well into my adult life. Having grown up poor, I believed that my value or self-worth stemmed from what car I drove, the clothes I wore, or how much money I made. None of these learned, unwarranted thought patterns are mine. They have nothing to do with who I am. I know these unauthorized thought patterns will always be there and will never go away. But if I don't feed into them, they will lie dormant and remain weak. I also know that if I give them the minutest bit of attention, I am off to the races! Bad choices start to look really tempting, and I have learned time and time again where that ends up.

Here is a more clinical version of how this thinking stacks up: As a young child, someone approves or disapproves of us based on our actions, and our first set of values and thinking begins to form. Add into the mix the media, peer pressure, bullying, rejection, social acceptance and so many of life's other experiences. Then, without realizing it, we've adopted someone else's beliefs or *unauthorized thought patterns*. Why do we act the way we do? Because we're conditioned to believe that such behavior gains acceptance and approval from others. And isn't that what most of us want, to be liked, accepted and validated by others? This desire drives us. We have this perfect, beautiful soul buried beneath layers of this preconditioned thinking, which was never ours to begin with! We are devoid of our true self.

Some people choose to live in that mindset, conditioned by external forces, while others will begin the process of peeling away these unauthorized thought patterns to discover their true self.

Do you remember the movie *Shrek?* Shrek, the ogre, explains to his friend, Donkey, "Ogres are like onions. They have layers." I couldn't agree more! People are like onions, too, our layers riddled with conditioned thinking and unauthorized thought patterns. If you peel away every layer of an onion, you'll eventually end up with nothing. It's only from this place of nothingness that we can be free of those patterns and thinking. It's also from here that you can see the truth needed to make the right choices and take the right actions. This truth helps you reach your full potential and create the life you deserve. But remember, this is a never-ending process, and one that must be worked on consistently throughout your life.

NEEDY AND GREEDY

It was 1969 and the *Summer of Love* was in full effect. I was 7 years old, living with my mama in what felt like a commune in the Haight-Ashbury in San Francisco. We lived in a two-bedroom apartment above a Chinese restaurant right on Haight Street. The parties never ended. An endless stream of strange people came and went. Drugs and alcohol were an everyday thing. The adults at these parties would often entertain themselves by blowing marijuana smoke in my face to see how it affected me. Later in life, I realized just how wrong this was.

The only good thing about this time was roller skating with Lillian, another 7-year-old who lived in the apartment with us. We liked to skate to an area famously known as "Hippie Hill" in Golden Gate Park. As we rolled up to it, we often could hear bands playing and see people running around naked, dancing. This was normal for the times. Little did I know that these weren't just any old bands. I would later come to learn that *Jimi Hendrix, Big Brother and the Holding Company* featuring *Janis Joplin*, and *Carlos Santana* were among the bands that played there. I still think those were some cool moments in my life, even though I did not know who they were at the time.

Every night, I slept in a queen-size bed in the apartment, between two older girls who were about 12. They would each pull the blanket we shared to their sides, stretching it out, which left me lying in the middle with the tent-blanket suspended about a foot above me. When the girls did this, I knew that *it* was about to happen. Each girl would take turns touching me on my private parts. They would also kiss me. At 7 years old, I did not really know what was happening. I would lay there, petrified. I could barely breathe. The girls would laugh and tell me it was all right. Deep down, I knew that what they were doing to me was not right. Later, in therapy, I learned that it was molestation.

At the age of 12, I had my first sexual intercourse with a girl who was 17. It happened at another one of those parties, in a rundown apartment in the Mission District of San Francisco, while my mother and a group of people slept only feet away. Again, I recall that feeling of not being able to breathe or move.

For me, these two traumatic life experiences would set in motion a pattern of promiscuous behavior that left a trail of one-night stands and broken relationships, accompanied by my deceit and lies. Add that my father had been married four times, and my mom left my dad for his best friend. Needless to say, my role models for healthy relationships were pretty thin.

I always say you can buy sex on a street corner, but you can't buy love or true intimacy. I recognized that as long I engaged with women purely for sex, I would remain unfulfilled. It became a bottomless pit of trying to fill an empty place in my heart with one woman after another.

Like a good addict looking for their next fix, as soon as I got it and the act of sex was over, I felt dirty and filled with regret, and wanted to leave. Sex by itself never led to wanting to get closer to a woman and spend the night with her. It was nothing more than instant gratification.

I hurt many kind and beautiful women on this path of self-destruction. I rationalized my choices and actions—I was just "sowing my oats." And because of my history, I was justified in my dysfunctional behavior. I was "Mr. Non-committal" and would have nothing to do with a relationship of real value. I cannot count the number of women I had sex with and how many tearful exits I orchestrated.

I eventually gave my lifestyle a name: "Needy and Greedy." I acted like a needy child, who in actuality was looking for love and intimacy. Unfulfilled, I constantly tried to feed the greedy monster that devoured every woman who crossed my sick path.

The sad part was that I knew my behavior was wrong, yet still chose to live this way. I understood perfectly well that insanity was making the same mistake over and over, while expecting different results. Still, in needy-and-greedy mode, I was a sick force to be reckoned with.

This lifestyle would dominate me for the better part of my life. I had even gone to *Sex Addicts Anonymous* thinking I had a mental condition. I sat in those meetings and listened to the stories, which made it even worse for me. Comparing myself to the other people in group only gave me more wiggle room to push the envelope to act out. I mean, I was not masturbating 36 times a day or spending every hard-earned dollar on prostitutes. And, if I wanted to find a steady supply of other like-minded needy-and-greedy people, those meetings were filled with them. So, my attendance was short-lived.

Things finally came to a head when I was 40. One night, I found myself dining in a Mexican restaurant with a good friend and his kids. Even though we all sat together, I was at a great distance from everyone at the table, lost inside my head, living in the insanity of yet another dysfunctional relationship that ended.

I share this moment because, as I sat there, I found myself at a crossroad. On one hand, I could be on a path to ending up one of those 60-year-old guys who combs their hair over the bald spot and drives what I called a "dick" car (any new and fast automobile that attracts the chicks) and chases twenty-something-year-old women to prove "I still got it." Or, at forty-something, was I ready to end the insanity of a lifetime in favor of something that had the potential to be meaningful and lasting?

The sound of the kids' laughter brought me back to the table and I caught the tail end of my friend's question, "Are you all right?" I halfheartedly nodded "yes," but knew it was a lie.

During this time, I also began to think about what another friend said to me: "Don't wait for the right woman to come along. Make yourself right, so you will be ready when she does." I played his statement like a broken record in my head, as I sat at that table in the restaurant. My purpose would become to make myself whole and right.

I stopped dating or I should say, "Sleeping around," altogether. I went on self-imposed celibacy for three years. I knew the journey to the right me was inward, not outward. I knew the hard work was all on me. I had to be willing to pull my own covers back and get honest with myself. I had to learn to love myself. I figured if I could do that, I could be vulnerable for someone to love me as I am. I was on a path to self-acceptance. I had to accept my past regressions. I had to accept responsibility for everyone I had hurt, especially the hurt I had done to myself. It was brutal for a while. I spent nights crying hard, lying with my face against the floor. I would beat myself up with the shame I felt for what I had done. I knew that the only way to get to the other side was by going through every emotion that went with it. I felt inside out, and totally exposed.

I began to discover the real me that was lost back in the summer of '69 in that apartment in the Haight. I did an exercise that I learned from a self-help book—one I found at a secondhand store where my mama and I bought used books. I visualized myself as an adult, going into that apartment and walking into that bedroom where I was first molested. There, I would find myself as a 7-year old boy sitting on the floor in a corner, crying. I would talk to my younger self, reassuring him and telling him that none of this was his fault. I would tell him that it was the fault of the people who molested him and that they had put the shame in his heart and mind. I promised Brannon The Boy that Brannon The Adult would protect him, and that he would never have to feel that hurt again. I would then take him by the hand and walk him out of that apartment into the light of a new day. I have done this exercise many times, and it has been very powerful in healing the wounded child inside of me.

Today, I realize I will always have needs. My commitment is never to let greed be my motivation and to fulfill only those needs that help me live my best life.

DR. V

Turning 30 became one of the turning points in my life. I had lived many lives so far; it was time for a change. This rite of passage from my twenties into a new decade was a chance to grow up. After a reckless youth, my inner self cried for change.

Meanwhile, one of my cousins, also in his thirties, had open-heart surgery for several blockages. I was freaked out, thinking it was a genetic thing and I could be next. I started to have chest pains, which I later learned were called "sympathy pains." It's like when a man whose partner is pregnant experiences some of the same symptoms and behavior as the woman, such as weight gain and morning sickness.

I made a visit to my doctor, who scheduled several tests. I was given an EKG and a treadmill stress test, and everything came up good. When the chest pains continued, my doctor recommended a psychiatrist.

As I sat in the waiting room, I had all these preconceived notions about what would go down. I wondered if this psychoanalysis stuff was real or just a crock of shit. I had this big chip on my shoulder because I didn't want this guy telling me that I was crazy. Although I knew it was my choice to be there, it didn't feel like it.

"The doctor will see you now," announced the receptionist. As I headed down the narrow corridor, the old me did not want to let go of my crazy life . But the moment I walked through the doctor's door, that life began to fade.

The old, judgmental tapes playing in my head were challenging me to check myself. I knew if I was going to get anything out of this, I would have to put down the gloves and be totally transparent with this guy.

A pudgy, middle-aged, pasty-white man greeted me with a limp handshake, and asked me to take a seat. I expected a couch like in the movies, but got a cold, vinyl chair left over from the '70s. My ass stuck to the chair, and it made these squeaky noises that sounded like farts. I didn't care because I did not want to be there in the first place. This inner conflict stayed with me through the first seven or eight sessions but, for some reason, I kept returning.

Doctor V was a quiet man with an easy, nonthreatening manner. He showed little emotion as he asked me questions.

"How does that make you feel?"

"Why do you feel that way?"

"What does that mean to you?"

At first, I didn't get Dr. V's line of questioning and where he was going with it. Nonetheless, I would suit up and show up, session after session, waiting for him to bestow some kind of wisdom, and declare me cured.

It was about the ninth visit when I understood why he always seemed to reply with a question. I got it. Dr. V was *not* there to give me the answers and fix me. He was there to help me become aware of myself. Through his inquiries, he guided me toward finding my own answers.

I responded to my martial arts students with a similar intention: "There isn't anything I can give you that you can't give yourself. You just have to be willing to take that journey inward. It can be lonely at times and you may not like what you see. But when you get to the other side, you'll be better for it."

It was time for me to practice what I preached. My time with Dr. V instilled a new confidence and maturity.

I sought Dr. V's help again after my sister Lisa died of heart failure at the age of 41 because I started to have similar chest pains to those I experienced when my cousin had had heart surgery. These felt much different, though. They were a deeper heartache.

I remember sharing this with Dr. V, who asked, "Have you ever heard of the term, 'a broken heart?'"

"Of course," I said. "I hear it all the time in all those sad love songs."

Dr. V said studies proved that people experienced physical heart pains when they suffered a traumatic loss, such as the death of a loved one or a bad breakup. I thought of the people who have been married almost their whole lives, where one spouse dies and the other soon follows.

"They die because of their broken hearts?" Dr V never replied to my question, if it even was a question. Maybe I was making a statement that I needed to say out loud to see the impact of emotions on my physical being.

Either way, it seemed like good medicine. I was clear that the way we think has an incredible affect on our physical body. In my own life, my thinking has elevated me to amazing heights at times. Other times, it has left me paralyzed, mentally and physically.

My time with Doctor Vogel reinforced my commitment to constantly learn, practice and master my thinking to become a better me.

Now, I look at my mind like a muscle, and exercise it by thinking *happy thoughts*. Thinking based upon gratitude and living in the present helps me cultivate a positive mindset.

I nourish my mind with healthy information to promote growth and keep it strong. I read everything I can relating to mastering one's self.

I write in a journal as a way of keeping my thoughts organized. It's a form of purging that lets me to empty my mind. It offers me clarity when I can see my thoughts written out on paper. When I have a good day, I can look back at my journal and see everything I did that to make it great. It gives me a step-by-step process to replicate the awesome days. When I have a bad day, I see what I have written and make sure not to repeat those behaviors.

I realize the world can often be filled with cynicism and negativity. If I am not mindful about what I allow into my thoughts, it can pollute my positivity. I have experienced this insanity firsthand by allowing someone else's ill-intended actions to affect me. And I find myself depressed if I watch too much TV news.

I live by a philosophy that goes by the acronym *CAL.* With every life situation, I have three choices: I can **C**hange it, **A**ccept it or **L**et it go. *CAL.* In theory, it sounds easy, but it never is.

If I can effect change on a circumstance that I would like to make better or different, I will exhaust every resource to do so. But I know that some things I cannot change, like the losses of my loved ones. My inability to realize I cannot change these situations has brought some of the greatest sadness and pain in my life.

That brings me to acceptance. Acceptance gives me peace. I have driven myself crazy with my unwillingness to accept life's terms. Denial that things are the way they are wreaks havoc.

The practice of acceptance is a most worthy life skill to master. I do so through prayer, journaling and the real knowing that I deserve to be happy. I am committed to seeing the world through the eyes of tolerance, understanding, patience and respect.

I also accept that suffering is a part of life. It is something we all go through; it is part of life's process. It is no greater or lesser than the things we enjoy in life, such as love, family and achieving goals. This perspective of *acceptance* has lifted much of the fear I used to associate with suffering.

The last choice is to *let it go.* At first, this practice made me feel totally defeated. Now, I find it liberating. *Letting go* is like purging or throwing up poison that your body just wants out. Letting go of people, situations and things that are toxic and harmful to my life is definitely a good thing.

In the evenings, *letting go* is my method of choice, and gets me through the night. It is not a perfect process, but I believe all roads lead to a higher self. When I am having one of those days, I just remember Dr. V's questions that challenged me to step up to the plate, aim high, and swing hard.

DON'T BELIEVE THE HYPE

Humility has taught me never to believe my own hype. Ego perpetuates the self-justification of bad habits and behavior that narrows my thinking and limits me in a fixed mindset. Entrenched, I know I'll miss out on living to my full potential.

I have a small circle of people who I trust will tell me when I am not doing my best. This is important to me because it's easy to become complacent. It is imperative for me to have that system of checks and balances, so I'm constantly growing and learning. I seek mentors who resonate with my values and inspire me by example.

On the flip side, I've got to look out for the haters and critics. It could be the littlest thing—a tweet, a post on Facebook, even my own *stinking thinking!* I am determined not to allow those negative thoughts to rent space in my head. Otherwise, I am screwed. The only way to guard myself is to stay away from negative people, places, things and actions that trigger and feed my unhealthy side.

My first stint as a martial arts school owner was in 1981, and lasted about nine months. I owned a school in Southern California where every night was fight night. Needless to say, it was short lived. I was taught from an early age that you either suffered for your art or sold out to become a "McDojo," where it was all about the money.

Almost 20 years later, with encouragement—and a small loan—from friends and family, I opened another martial arts school in San Francisco. While my school grew, I still believed I had to suffer for my art. Five years into the business, I found myself in the emergency room, once again injured while training. This time, I had a cut above my left eye. While sparring in class, I had walked into an elbow when I threw a left hook.

I distinctly remember being asked by the friend who accompanied me to the hospital, "How long are you going to keep doing this?"

"What do you mean? I've done this since I was 5. Fighting is all I know."

"You can't win in this situation," my friend said. "If you hurt somebody, you look bad. If they hurt you, you look even worse."

In the days that followed, I was reminded of my friend's question each time I looked in the mirror and saw the stitches above my eye. I realized that if I was to be successful in every aspect of my life, I needed to clearly define my purpose to create win-win situations. I never believed in the business philosophy that to win, someone must lose.

I went through this process without involving my ego—and found that my true purpose was to serve others. I wanted to take the martial arts that helped me be my best, use it to change others' lives, and have an impact on the community. This could only happen if I checked my ego, and stopped thinking I knew everything. I learned I am not afraid of what I don't know. It's the things I know that sometimes cloud my vision and my capacity to learn and grow. When I stopped learning, my life and business became stagnant. And what good is stagnant water? It's undrinkable and becomes a breeding ground for parasites.

The ego is a dangerous animal. It rationalizes and feeds that hype with self-justification, self-will and selfishness. So, it's important to practice humility. Humility teaches me that I can always do and be better. Humility keeps me hungry for knowledge. It keeps me from believing my own hype. I am my own best friend and I am my own worst enemy. When I start believing my own lies—when I rationalize my beliefs, behavior and choices—then, guess what? I stop evolving and making the effort to better myself.

I like to think of myself as the oldest living white belt. Just as my beginning students, I put that belt on every day, with the intent to be the best version of me. This practice, of learning greater humility and not believing my own hype, have resulted in two successful martial arts schools, a consulting and mentoring service, and several prospering online businesses. I do this by living my purpose and maintaining integrity. It goes with serving people at the highest level, where everyone can win. And most importantly, I don't believe any of the hype.

THE HOMELESS HISTORY TEACHER

I was getting out of my car one day when a man approached me. By the nature of his clothing and the shopping cart he was pushing, he appeared homeless. I wasn't in the most desirable part of town, so I found the *ghetto* in me stepped up as he got closer. The man asked, "Sir, could you possibly spare some change?" I was floored by how articulately he spoke. I put my guard down, and found myself intrigued by his demeanor. I had a bag of change in my back seat that I intended to redeem at one of those coin machines. In that moment, I decided to put it to better use.

I said, "I have a bag of coins in the back seat of my car that I will give you right now, if you would be willing to give me a few minutes of your time and talk with me."

At first, this vagabond gave me a really weird look, but when he saw the bag I produced as proof, he quickly accepted my invitation.

I leaned against my car, as this guy steadied himself by holding onto the handle of his shopping cart. I inquired, "You speak really well and you seem to have it together, so I can't help but wonder how you ended up homeless?" As he paused and took a deep, measured breath, I had the feeling that he was about to enlighten me. He seemed to grip the handle on his cart a bit tighter with one hand as he raised the other one and pointed upward. He exclaimed, "I use to be a high school history teacher. I had a home mortgage, property taxes and many other expenses. I was part of the rat race, chasing the cheese like everyone else. I was conditioned to believe what defined success from every TV commercial and ad I read in the newspaper. One day, I sat down and did the math. I was in debt and realized I would always be in debt until the day I died, based upon what a teacher makes. I started considering what my options were to what I viewed as a dead-end existence. After doing the homework, I learned that living in San Francisco was the best place to be homeless. I could panhandle and earn, on average, one hundred dollars a day. If I did it five days a week, I could clear tax free about two thousand dollars a month. There are plenty of homeless shelters here, so I could always find a place to lay down my head. During the day when they closed down and you had to vacate, I could go to the library, movies, or just go on a walkabout around this beautiful city by the bay. As long as I was in line at a shelter by 5 o'clock, I was certain to get a cot for that night. If I missed out, I could still afford a few dollars to rent a room if I had to. The weather here never gets too bad, so, worst case scenario, if I had to sleep on the street, I could always find shelter in a doorway or ride the buses all night. So, when I counted my pennies, I could actually make more money being homeless. I have way less stress and none of the demands that go with being the so-called 'responsible and productive member of society.' My time is all my own and I don't have to answer to anybody. Heck, I don't even have to pay taxes! So, at the end of the day, I am much happier this way than I have ever been."

I stood there, dumbfounded. Everything this homeless guy said made perfect sense. He had figured out what success was for him. It wasn't about keeping up with the Joneses, making more money, having a bigger house, a better car, and all the debt and interest that go with it. This history teacher had defined what life and happiness meant to him. He didn't care what anyone thought or how people viewed him. Their opinion or judgment did not factor into the choices he made to create the life that gave him joy. This man, without a roof over his head, danced to his own tune and, from everything he professed, he was at peace with his decision.

As he walked away with my bag of change, I found myself in reflection. I began questioning my every action and motive for the life I was living or, in this case, the one I should have been living. I played our conversation over in my mind. I understood everything he said. It even made sense in some ways. I still could not wrap my head around someone choosing to live on the streets.

Then, one night, as I was sitting by the fireplace playing my guitar, I had one of those moments of clarity. I was stuck in the stereotypical thinking he spoke of. He had said, "Don't believe everything you see on TV or read in the newspapers." I feel what he was really saying was, "Don't behave like sheep being led to slaughter, blind to the truth that lives inside us." This homeless guy may have been without a physical home but he was far from destitute. He discovered how to be a critical thinker without outside influences. His home was in his heart, and he took it into every shelter and onto every street corner where he panhandled.

The lessons I learned from the *Homeless History Teacher* still influence my life today. They led me to challenge the status quo and walk a path all my own. I am the first to raise my hand and ask a question when something doesn't seem right. This teacher may be destitute by societal standards, but in my eyes, he was rich. And the amazing thing about it all was that it only cost me a bag of change.

NINE CROWNS

"How many crowns does that make now?" I asked my dentist. She looked down at my chart and I could see her using a pen to count the number from my X-rays. It took a while. My doctor finally looked up and sympathetically replied, "Nine."

Funny, I don't even remember getting the first crown. I do remember being about 10 years old when my father took my sisters and me to the dentist for what seemed like the first time. What stays with me most from that memory was how upset the dentist was with my father. By the condition of our teeth, they had obviously been neglected. He showed my father an X-ray of several of my molars that had more cavity than tooth left in them, which was a sign that the decay had gone unchecked for too long. He looked at me with concern, asking if I brushed my teeth every day. I didn't know what to say and simply looked to my father. The doctor was visibly upset as he turned away and signaled to his assistant to prepare me for some much-needed dental work.

This experience began my quest over the next 40 years to repair the damage and improve the health of my teeth. Some days when I am sitting in the dentist's chair, my mouth reminds me of my impoverished childhood. I will never forget how I was afraid to tell my father how badly my teeth were aching, because his reaction was always that of irritation for having to take time out of his schedule to take one of us to see the dentist. Today, I understand it was more his shame and frustration of not having the means to pay for it. He could have applied for medical aid from the city and county, but my father was a proud man. He would never ask for anything that appeared to be a handout.

I have also had two root canals and one implant because of my poor dental health. Lastly, I have worn a night-guard for the better part of 15 years. Well, the night-guard is now a wire-meshed version, because I have chewed through several of the hard-plastic night-guards with my excessive grinding. Grinding my teeth goes beyond the standard medical reason associated with stress. I also grind my teeth from all the years of wearing a mouthpiece as a fighter. Every time I would punch or kick in a competition or training, I would bite down on my mouthpiece to help generate more force upon impact. Also, when an opponent hit or kicked me in the face, I would clench down to absorb the shock. Fighting by itself can also be traumatic. As a result, grinding my teeth has become a habit.

What is important about this episode is how I have learned to manage my stress and its effects. I have learned that stress is an emotion that can be mastered. It requires a disciplined practice that begins with the acceptance that the burdens of life are something we all carry. I embrace stress like my best friend because if I ignore it, it can consume me in darkness and anxiety.

I manage the physical effects of tension through martial arts training, getting proper sleep, weekly massages and eating right most days.

I practice meditation, where I breathe in and say to myself, "I am breathing." This is important because, if I was not breathing, I probably wouldn't be stressed at all right?" Next, I breathe out and say, "I am grateful I get to live my best life." I then repeat this process and go through a gratitude list, which includes my family, health, career, friends, success and more. This practice offers me a deep sense of calm and serenity.

Living in the present moment gives me an upper hand in dealing with stress. I believe that is why the "present" is called just that, because it is truly *a gift*. But if I choose to do anything less, and please pardon the visual, it's like having one foot in yesterday and one foot in tomorrow and I'm peeing all over today. Got the picture?

Yesterday is but a memory and tomorrow is a dream. If I can be *right here*, *right now*, I can appreciate everything *the present* offers. It relieves any anxiety I may feel, and gives me peace.

I make it a practice never to get too tired, hungry or lonely. Finding myself in any of those states gets me pretty stressed out. Too tired and hungry are obvious, but too lonely needs explanation. There is a big difference between being alone and being lonely. I relish my alone time. It creates a balance in my demanding world. But if I choose to isolate, it takes me to an ugly and desperate place. We all need human contact. We are not meant to go through life alone. I make it a priority to surround myself with quality family and friends who I can reach out to when needed.

Most importantly, I have a deep spiritual faith. It helps me remain positive through the hardships of life. When I feel the effects of stress overwhelming me, I let go and turn it over to God. I don't have to carry all of life's heavy burdens. It gives me a feeling that everything will be all right. And through God's love and mercy, not only will I be able to effectively manage my stress, I just might get to keep what healthy teeth I have left. Can I get an "amen" to that?

A LEARNING MINDSET

I find that an important part of my happiness is living from a "white belt" or "learning mindset. I've been practicing the martial arts for more than 50 years, and hold the rank of eighth-degree black belt, but have always believed the belt simply holds up my pants. I stand by the philosophy, "Always a student and never a master." I always have something to learn, right? I love to learn, and never really cared about appearing smart. The teacher could count on me to be the first in class to raise my hand and ask a question. I figured if I was a good learner, I would become smarter in the process. This philosophy promotes growth on all fronts, and I am dedicated to the process.

This learning *mindset* is based on the intent to be a better version of me each day. I do so with a clearly defined set of core values, such as integrity, discipline and respect. I apply these to any situation I face. My goal is not to be *too set in my ways* because it hinders my ability to learn what I need from that situation. It can stop me from gaining the right information that could lead me to a better me.

To cultivate the learning and growth to live to my full potential, my thinking must remain fluid, not fixed. A fluid mindset grows by choice, habit and action. It evolves from recognizing the bad habits that inhibit growth and replacing them with good ones. A *Learning Mindset* is about clearly defining my core values and realizing my purpose in this world. Again, this mindset is a way of thinking that is in a constant state of flux. It is ever fluid like water, with the disposition to learn, adapt and grow with life's many challenges, to overcome them and become a better person.

That is why I make the constant effort to create and live in a mindset where I can always do better and be a better person. It promotes the desire to learn constantly, and is crucial to facilitating growth.

A *mindset of complacency* has the opposite effect. It narrows my vision into believing that my way is the only way, and that the world has nothing to teach me. This mindset is debilitating and inhibits my growth because it is fed by ego and insecurity.

A *Learning Mindset* also offers me the best potential to succeed. It lets me to see things from many perspectives, not just my own. It provides me with valuable input and varied information to help me form beliefs and make the right choices. This mindset promotes constant growth, which is in alignment with the person I aspire to be.

For me, making the change to a *growth* or *learning mindset* took peeling away several unhealthy core beliefs. It didn't happen all at once. My peeling away of these beliefs and the behaviors that went with them happened over time—it was a series of life experiences that showed me the way to get to the next level of being a better me. I say it all the time, "I do some of my best learning and growing lying flat on my face."

A *growth* or *learning mindset* is a choice. With every life experience, good or bad, I make the choice whether to be negatively affected by those experiences or to learn from them. What best facilitates this for me is to practice being humble. It encourages me to embrace all of life's experiences as opportunities to learn and grow, which then helps influence the person I strive to be.

Having grown up with little, humility came easy to me. Some would call it "humble beginnings," but we just called it "poor." Having to wear secondhand clothing, not getting presents on Christmas most years, and never celebrating our birthdays, my sisters and I knew how to be humble. There was no room for ego in our impoverished environment.

Today, I have taken what some would view as the short end of the stick in life, and have worked it to my advantage. Because I grew up with so little, it is easy for me to be grateful for what I have. I embrace the simple pleasures in life and am easily appreciative of the smallest things people do for me.

My mindset is in a constant state of change, and I choose where it will sit from moment to moment. I accept that I am not responsible for what happens to me but I am responsible for how I choose to act on it. My desire is to base all my decisions on a healthy foundation of learning. That is why it is so important to commit to learning and practicing life skills for a healthy mindset. It enables me to live in balance consistently, regardless of circumstances.

A *learning mindset* is also a *balanced mindset*—founded on the equal enrichment of the mind, body and spirit; this is the only way to find sustainable happiness. This balance recognizes that the way to happiness is the journey inward, where my true self lives. This self is free of all the preconditioned beliefs and values fed to me from outside influences. My commitment to a *balanced mindset* is where happiness lives. It allows me to reach my full potential.

Consider the holiday classic, *A Christmas Carol.* Scrooge was miserable and disconnected from humanity because he was so consumed by greed and his past fears. "Bah, humbug!" was Scrooge's response to everything positive. But then Scrooge was made to reflect on his past, present and future to help him learn that he was wasting his life and missing out on true happiness and the joy of giving.

A *learning mindset* is about living free from the past, without fear of an unknown future, and to be fully present in the moment. I remind myself constantly that the *present* is called just that because it's a *gift*. Being grateful for every bit of life we are given, challenges and all, takes incredible courage and yields phenomenal results.

Someone who is learning is happier than someone who believes they have nothing left to learn. I believe that if I am learning, I am growing. If I am growing, I am living, and that makes me happy!

Mind, body and spirit,
The three elements
That make up the
Sum of one's being.
One must feed
Each element equally
To maintain the balance
Necessary to sustain
A life of symmetry.
If just one of these
Elements is neglected,
One's being will be
Out of balance,
Feeding into
Addictive behavior.
So, maintain your
Mind, body and spirit
To walk an honest path
Of achieving true
Peace within.

FACING FEAR WITH FAITH

Faith is maintaining a positive mindset in a sometimes negative and cynical world. I still believe good always conquers evil, that the underdog will emerge victorious, and the tortoise will always beat the hare. If I never give up and always do my best, I have faith that I can succeed at most things. I was never the biggest or strongest fighter, but my heart and determination made me a champion many times over.

Whatever our spiritual journey, faith will help us reach our full potential. Faith is hope without fear...the trust that a happy ending is just around the corner, where we'll find the beginning of endless possibilities. Faith is the strength to hold on and hang in there when all we want to do is give up. Faith challenges us to give when we feel like we have so little. Faith is love beyond fear. Faith is that precious, childlike moment when we honestly believe that peace is the path we deserve to walk. So, don't give up five minutes before the miracle. If we are determined and stay the course, we can do most anything!

Research has proven that people with some type of faith recover from surgical procedures better and quicker than those without. This is just one of the amazing aspects the power faith has to influence our lives.

Fear is a real emotion. All of us are afraid of something. Sometimes, I am afraid of not being able to provide for my family. At other times, I am afraid of getting ill and not being able to work. I am afraid of losing the people I love so dearly. I am afraid of not being able to live up to the standards I teach. But what gives me peace and the ability to face my fears on a daily basis is my faith in God. He teaches me I am right where I am supposed to be. I trust that God never gives me more than I can handle. With God, I have the strength to face all my fears and strive to be a better person. It is an act of true faith to believe everything will be all right. When my fears get the best of me, I surrender them to God. I believe that where I can't, God can, so I choose to "Let go and let God," as the saying goes.

And I choose to embrace my fears like a best friend. I hold them close to my heart with acceptance and love. This helps me overcome any shame or feelings of being inadequate for having those fears to begin with.

Lastly, I accept that it's OK to be afraid. (However, it isn't all right to allow my fears to stop me from fulfilling my dreams and creating the best life possible.) I pray that, with faith, hope and trust in God's love and mercy, I can overcome my fears and live to my full potential.

SURRENDER

To find peace and balance, it's important to accept life on life's terms. When I don't do this...when I resist life's unpredictable journey...I find myself in some dark places. It's vital to accept that I am not in control of other people and circumstances. When I surrender to this fact, I can begin to take responsibility for myself. I know this is always easier said than done, but acceptance of these things is a vital key to letting go of the past.

Why is it that we don't try to control the seasons? We have no problem accepting that the seasons are out of our control. So why don't we choose to look at the rest of our lives this way? We cling to the illusion that we are actually in control of life. Try not going to the bathroom for 24 hours and show me how much control you have.

I've learned that I am not in control, while knowing that I am responsible for how I choose to perceive, embrace and process everything that happens—or doesn't—in my life.

Bruce Lee said, "You put water into a cup, it becomes the cup. You put water into a bottle and it becomes the bottle. You put water in a teapot and it becomes the teapot. Water can flow or it can crash. Be water, my friend." Although this philosophy is simple, it's often quite difficult to apply. Many of us are rigid in our conditioned thinking, to the point that we are not teachable. This rigid thinking makes us like stagnant water, and what good is that? That water that was once meant to nourish and cleanse us is now poisonous.

The key is to accept life on life's terms, to *surrender*. John Lennon said it best in his song *Beautiful Boy*, "Life is what happens to you while you're busy making other plans."

> I find myself
> In transition, again,
> "In flux," one might say,
> Crossing bridges and
> Ascending stairs
> To the next level
> Or plateau as far as
> Experiences go.
> The only strategy
> Is patience and faith.
> Just be.
> Being is the answer.
> Do not think or
> Act with emotion.

Simply be.
Exist on a level
Of harmony and
Inner peace will
Light the way
Through the darkness
Of fearful confusion.

SPIRITUALITY

Spirituality is the foundation of my life. It defines my purpose and core values. It's the tool that helps me build a life of good choices and right actions.

As I've already shared, spirituality wasn't always my first choice. I have made the mistake of inflicting my self-will repeatedly in my life, only to find myself on my knees, defeated. I am only challenged when I choose to make the same mistakes over and over, while expecting different results, which is insanity (attributed to Einstein).

Another key element to spirituality is my ability to let go of self-will and have faith. Understanding and having faith are very personal journeys for each of us. Investing in my spiritual growth is essential to my happiness. I share this passionately with anyone looking for fulfillment.

I don't know about you, but sometimes I have an uncanny ability to rationalize my own bad behavior and thinking. I end up with this warped perception and believe my own lies. That is why I turn to spiritual practice instead of my own devices. When I don't, I find myself in a state of fear and doubt. I have come to label this state of turning to my own devices as "fear-based thinking"—rigidly adhering to entrenched beliefs based on my past and self-justification for holding these beliefs—which leads me to being egotistical and acting as if the universe should revolve around me. I cannot entertain a better version of me and move forward without my faith.

Fear-based thinking also stops me from doing my best work, which is to serve the greater good and strive to better humanity. It has taken great humility and rigorous honesty to accept this powerful truth that self-will is faithless and fear-based, and then to let go of it in faith.

HUMILITY

Sometimes, when we hear the word *humility*, it is perceived as being *humiliated*. But what *humility* really means is to be modest or humble. It challenges us to act without ego and recognize that we are all equal.

We can practice humility by acting and speaking out of love, not fear. Fear-based actions are the opposite of true humility. Fear postures, dominates, growls and wants the upper hand. When we act out of love, we are balanced, complete and at peace amid the chaos of life. This journey of humility isn't always easy because, as we all know, life has a way of humbling us when we least expect it.

Practicing humility—learning to be mindful—has nothing to do with being humiliated. It encourages us to be perfect in our imperfections. It asks us to look at so-called "failures" as opportunities to learn and grow. To act with a humble heart allows us the courage to take chances, make mistakes, and learn the things we need to be a better person. It is often through our mistakes that we do our greatest learning. Fear of being criticized for our mistakes keeps us from taking chances (there is that fear-based thinking again).

The negative connotations of humility are shame and weakness. However, true humility is quite the opposite! Humility is strength and poise, calm and control. Humility acts out of love rather than reacting in fear. Humility leads by example and does not boast or demand attention. Many influential people, such as Martin Luther King Jr., Mother Teresa and Mahatma Gandhi, are excellent demonstrations of the power of humility.

Humility is the foundation of a positive mindset and helps promote life balance. As Mac Davis sings, "Oh Lord, it's hard to be humble." This lyric is an expression of an ego-based mindset that is rooted in the insecurity and fear of being perceived as inadequate. This ego-based mindset feeds on and into our insecurities and, if unchecked, will leave us fixed, paralyzed, stagnant, judgmental, self-loathing and narrow-minded. The ego-based mindset is the antithesis of a *Growth Mindset*.

LIVE A QUALITY LIFE

We can wake to a new day, healthy and strong. We can live lives filled with relationships we value greatly and invest in. If we choose to see our lives through the eyes of gratitude, no matter how challenging life can be, we will witness the many miracles it offers us to be our best.

We all deserve to live a quality life. So how do we achieve it? Again, this is relevant to the individual and how they define *quality life*. To recap, here are a few absolutes that I practice passionately:

- Start and end each day in spiritual reflection through prayer and meditation.
- Practice an attitude of gratitude each morning by expressing appreciation for everyone and everything in life.
- Never get too tired, too hungry, or too lonely. Sleep, eat, exercise and surround myself with quality people.

- Never forget that I was once a child. Play as much as life allows.
- Hang out with children every chance I get. They are some of life's greatest teachers.
- Practice the *Law of Abundance* by believing that I'll always have enough.
- Keep my morning routine the same so I can focus my energy on creating a positive mindset to have the best day.
- Spend quality time alone to appreciate myself.
- Read every day, because learning is the key to success.
- Practice accepting life on life's terms knowing that it is the path to serenity.
- Do nothing sometimes; it promotes work-life balance.
- Don't take anything personally; not everything is about me.
- Sing because it feeds my soul and makes me happy.
- Practice the philosophy of "paying it forward," by giving without expecting anything.

- Be nonjudgmental, loving and forgiving toward others and myself.
- Be still, meditate and breathe mindfully every day.
- Practice being present in the moment, for it is truly a gift.
- Embrace change; it is inevitable.
- Always keep my word and do what I say I'm going to do.
- Learn and practice having good morals and values.
- Spend quality time with family and friends.
- Make mistakes every day, but don't make the same ones.
- Say, "I'm sorry" and "I love you" as much as is needed to keep me humble and appreciative.
- Always do my best and never give up.
- Keep a journal because "If I can see it, I can be it." By writing things down, I get a clear picture of what is needed to be a better version of myself each day.

IT WORKS WHEN YOU WORK IT

"It works when you work it, so work it because you're worth it," or so the Alcoholics Anonymous saying goes. What resonates with me is the "because you're worth it" part. I must first decide that *I am worth it* to have the courage to make the changes in my life that will make it better.

Self-sabotage, based on obsolete core beliefs, is the biggest reason I experienced limited success in my life. I would sabotage what success I gained by making excuses for why I didn't want it. Today, I know my dysfunctional childhood played a big part in my self-defeating attitude. It taught me that I was not deserving of the best life had to offer. Recognizing self-sabotage is an even bigger challenge, because it's easy to rationalize that I was a product (or victim) of that environment. It doesn't take a whole lot of courage to climb onto a pity pot and cry, "Poor me, poor me!" The real work began when I recognized that the way I was thinking wasn't serving my best interests today.

So how do I do this? It's probably not what you'd expect. Rather than feeling guilt or shame—or getting angry and beating myself up—I embraced those old core beliefs like my best friend. It was only from this point of love that I begin to heal and change. If I chose to run and hide, I'd be giving into the fear, and it would own me like it had in the past. I had to bring that *stinking thinking* into the light of a new day if I was to overcome and heal.

It's futile to resist change. Change is guaranteed. What causes me the most pain is fighting change when change is needed. Holding on to old beliefs that were established in my childhood have no legitimate place in my life today. The only value that they have is to serve as lessons or calls to action, to shape and model new behaviors on a path to success.

So, I work it because I am worth it. I work hard to build my self-esteem, never giving up and always doing my best. I can be confident that this really does work when I work at it consistently. And that means working harder than anyone I know. I work it without excuses, blame, or finger pointing. I hold myself accountable for my every thought, word and action. I know it is my space and my race, and it is up to me to create a life worth living.

NEVER GIVE UP

I often get weary and feel like giving up. At these moments, it helps me to remember that God never hands me any more than I can handle. This gives me hope and helps me embrace the day. Frequently, I say to myself, "Brannon, it is easy to be great when things are going your way. But can you be great when things are difficult? That is what builds character. That is what makes me a better person." But sometimes, in the middle of life's challenges, that philosophy goes right out the window.

When this happens, I utilize many of the martial arts skills I have learned throughout my 50 years of training. Discipline and focus keep me fully engaged in the moment. The practice of controlling my emotions inspires me to take the right actions. I maintain life balance by continuing to learn every day, exercising and eating healthily, and pursuing the things about which I am most passionate. I remember I was once a kid and never take anything too seriously. And I always call upon the people I love and trust to help me through these times. Tough times humble me and remind me that I never have to go through it alone. Being lonely is not a healthy place to be. Now there is a big difference between being *alone* and being *lonely*. I like being *alone* to read a good book, go for a walk, or write. I am *lonely* when I isolate myself from everyone else and am in a state of self-loathing. I feel sorry for myself, which can spiral downward into a state of depression. I can dig myself a hole so deep that I find myself looking up in despair with no possible way to get out.

When this happens, I surrender. I surrender, but I don't give up. I turn to God to lift me above my own limited thinking. Journey's song, *Don't Stop Believin'*, starts playing in my head. Before I know it, with God's love and mercy, I am out of that dark hole and standing with sunshine on my face.

POSITIVE THINKING IS CRUCIAL

In a world filled with so much sadness and negativity, it is crucial to have a positive attitude. Positive thinking is the key to overcoming the fear that negative thinking promotes. We have all said or thought at some time or another, "I can't..." and "I hate..." But that kind of thinking is "stinking thinking." It ensures failure right from the get-go. *Stinking Thinking* says, "You are not good enough, so why even try?" It is this fear that paralyzes us. It stops us from taking chances and excelling beyond our own complacency.

I choose to live by the mantra, "Yes, I can." And I encourage you to join me in this. And on those days where we don't believe we can, we can fake it until we make it. We can pretend to feel positive and, the next thing we know, we'll feel better. To reference *Star Wars,* in the spirit of a true Jedi master, do not allow the dark side to consume and dominate your thinking. We must do battle with negativity every day. We must not ignore *Stinking Thinking* because it will only fester and grow stronger. We can embrace the fear that negative thinking breeds, as if it were our best friend. We can invite fear to come out and play in the light of a positive day. Let's say, "Yes, I can!" each and every day to see the endless possibilities of greatness that we all possess. Come on, now. Let's say it together. "Yes, I can!" Say it again. "Yes, I can!" Don't you feel better now?

Round one-thousand,
Eight-hundred, thirty-two,
Brannon vs. Self-doubt.
Self-doubt has dominated
The early rounds but the
Tide seems to be turning.
Brannon's corner has advised him
To quit fighting Self-doubt
And embrace it like a best friend.
This left his opponent
Confused in the later rounds
And the momentum is changing.
Brannon is on his toes,
Bobbing, weaving and sticking
Self-doubt with explosive jabs
Of positive reinforcement.
He knows he can win this fight
With self-acceptance
And be a true champion.
Ladies and gentlemen,
Self-doubt is down for the count!
In a flurry of love,
Brannon has knocked out
Self-doubt to win
The *Championship of Self-Worth*.

CREATE A POSITIVE ATTITUDE

A smile and a positive attitude are the traits of a successful person. When we smile, we feel better and attract positive people into our lives. When we smile, the challenges we face will be easier. Exuding a positive attitude will inspire others. People will want to be around us.

To create a positive attitude, we must eliminate three words from our vocabulary—"problem," "try," and "should." To create a positive attitude, we can replace "problem" with "challenge," "try" with "do," and "should" with "will."

We can see difficult situations as challenges, not problems. Viewing difficult situations as challenges allows us to see them as *goals*. And having goals is inspiring. We'll be more motivated to achieve a successful outcome when we view problems as challenges.

Trying ensures failure at the outset. *Trying* lacks conviction. Again, Yoda told Luke Skywalker, "Do or do not. There is no try." *Trying* is a feeble excuse to rationalize our behavior and failure by saying, "At least, I tried." Successful people achieve their goals by *doing*, not *trying*.

How many times in our life have we said, "I *should* do that?" I *should* exercise more. I *should* eat better. I *should* change my job, etc.? Let's eliminate *should* from our vocabulary and replace it with *will*. I *will* work out regularly. I *will* eat better. I *will* set goals and achieve them. *I will* is an immediate call to action, and very motivating.

CHANGE HAPPENS

One thing you are guaranteed in life is change. Change is a constant and inevitable. Fighting change doesn't work. Instead, we can accept change and embrace the unknown with the smile of a child. We can't change people, places or things. We can only be responsible for changing ourselves. When we accept this, our intentions will be better served. Nothing ever stays the same. Just when we get use to something, it changes to something else. Change is the ability to be fluid, where rigid thinking would break under the stress. When we welcome change, we open the door to the unlimited opportunities that come with it.

HELPLESS BUT NOT HOPELESS

My wife and I rushed our 4-year-old son Brayden to the emergency room with a severe croup attack. While there, he stopped breathing and went Code Blue. His lips were blue; his eyes rolled back in his head; and his little body shook violently. I remember when the attending doctor called out, "Code Blue!" I thought my son was dying.

Everything was so chaotic as the staff worked frantically to get Brayden breathing and stabilized. I stepped back and found myself rocking side to side with my hands in prayer. Nothing could describe my feeling of complete helplessness. All my wisdom and life experiences were useless as I watched my son lie there motionless, as they tended to him. I stood there with nothing, unable to console my wife as she cried, witnessing our son's unreal situation unfold. I could not believe that just hours before, we were playing in the park and everything was fine. Now, here we were, and my son was not breathing. At this moment, I truly understood the meaning of feeling helpless.

The medical team in the emergency room stabilized Brayden and told us they needed to transport him to a pediatric ICU in San Francisco. They said an ambulance and team would be en route shortly. My wife decided it would be best for her to go home, grab some things, and arrange for our nanny to care for our daughter, Teya. Meanwhile, I was not leaving my son's side until he returned home safe and whole.

Fast forward 70 hours, and the doctors said Brayden was past the worst. He was still in the pediatric ICU with pneumonia in both lungs and had a viral infection in his throat. He was no longer in an induced coma and is was slowly coming off the many medications I could not pronounce. He was still having difficulties breathing but was improving by the hour.

During those three dark days, where minutes felt like hours of uncertainty, I fought to find a new meaning of hope. In my heart and mind, there was no way my son was going to die. I would not and could not believe or accept that. The only option was to search for a belief unlike anything I had ever had before. Fear taunted and tested me as I watched my son lying there in the induced coma. Fear challenged me to abandon my faith and accept the worse outcome possible. But I would not give in to my fears. Every breath I took was filled with hopeful prayer that my son and I were going to walk out of that hospital together.

I recall on the third or fourth day, my wife telling me I should go outside and get some fresh air. But like I said, I was not leaving my son's side. My wife can be very convincing at times, though, and I found myself walking down California Street to get a cup of tea. At a distance, I could see a homeless man, sitting on the sidewalk asking passers-by for spare change. As I approached him, he stared at me in silence. He gave me a look as if I was the one who needed a handout.

I saw my reflection in a store window and found myself face to face with a stranger, weathered and beaten down. I hadn't showered in days, my hair was matted and I had on the same clothes I wore when I first entered the ER. Though fear had turned me inside out and I looked like shit, at least I was standing.

I got that much-needed cup of chai, and found solace on a bench, figuring I would blend in with the street people. I sat there, looking into my cup for answers. My innocent son did nothing to deserve this. And where was God while all of this was going on?

I believe I found my answer in about my ninth sip of tea. A deep calm washed over me as the hot liquid slid down my throat. I realized that the sun was shining and my son was still alive. I understood at that moment what hope or real faith was all about. It was to believe in something that could not be seen or proven. In my son's case, it was knowing without any doubt that he was going to be fine, even as he lay in that hospital bed at his worst. I could feel that God's love and mercy had been with my family and me throughout the past few days. I admit it was hard to see God through the fear and helplessness. In gratitude, I closed my eyes and raised my chin to receive the warmth of the sun.

I remember finishing my tea and walking into the nearest convenience store. I bought a disposable razor, a travel-size container of shaving cream, and some other toiletries for cleaning up. I decided my outside needed to match what I was feeling inside.

I found one of the hospital bathrooms and set about my task. I bathed in the sink, shaved, brushed my teeth and fixed myself up the best I could. My wife brought me a change of clothes, and I put those on, as well. The whole time I was cleansing, I was experiencing the hope that had found me on that bench with my cup of tea.

I share this experience with you because I want you to know that hope is the only thing that gave my family and me the strength to see this through. It steadied me through the storm of circumstance and uncertainty. Hope held my hand and gave me the courage to be there for my family, knowing Brayden was going to be OK. Even in my darkest moments of this ordeal, it was my unrelenting belief that calmed my heart and gave me peace.

So, yes, at moments like this, I will humbly accept that I am often helpless and must accept life's terms. I also accept that with hope, I can live my best life when it appears to be at its worst. I am reminded that even when I am helpless, I am never hopeless.

I'M GOING TO DIE, AREN'T I?

My mother's boyfriend was on the other end of the line. "Your Mama's pretty bad off, and in the hospital. You need to come here now." I knew this call would come one day. The news sounded so far away and disconnected from everything else on that March day.

My plane landed in Tucson at 1:30 in the morning. Oddly, one of the memories that stuck with me was the lime-green convertible Mustang the rental company gave me. I just stared at it in the parking stall. Everything felt surreal, as I climbed in and drove to the hospital.

The main entrance to the hospital closed at midnight, so I had entered through the emergency entrance. After a couple of inquiries, several elevators and a maze of hallways, I found my mama's room, and entered. She was sleeping. As I stood next to her bed, I reached out to hold her hand. My mama felt so sad and broken. She appeared much older than the last time I saw her, a few years prior. I kissed her forehead and she woke up.

"Hey, Mama," I said like I had so many times during the daily phone calls I would make to check on her.

She asked me what I was doing there, and I replied, "I am here to take care of you, Mama."

Shortly thereafter, the physician on duty came in and asked to speak with me out in the hall. As we stood there, he explained my mother's grave condition. She had dementia, sepsis (blood poisoning), gangrene, and her major organs were beginning to shut down. Basically, the doctor was informing me that my mama was going to die.

Mama had put me in charge after her stroke several years back, in case she became incapacitated. And now I had to choose whether to prolong the inevitable with life support or simply let her expire naturally. The latter would mean putting her in a hospice, where they would make her as comfortable as possible until she passed. Either way, I had to accept my mama was going to die.

My first response was that I wanted nothing to do with this situation. I did not want to decide if my mama was going to live. I realize my reaction was selfish, but I was overwhelmed and not ready for the responsibility of this choice. As the doctor walked away to leave me to process the information, I found myself praying, asking God for strength and guidance.

Everything felt heavy as I walked back into my mama's room. She was awake, sitting up and alert. She looked at me with a sense of clarity and said, "I'm going to die, aren't I?"

Before I could decide how to respond, I found myself at the end of the sentence, "Yes you are, Mama."

She grabbed my hand and stated with total peace, "Well, you know what to do; that's why I put you in charge."

I felt guilty because inside all I wanted to do was get back on a plane and go home to San Francisco. My mama was the one dying, yet she was the one at peace. I was still struggling to comprehend why anyone would put another person in charge of how and when he or she should exit this world.

I just looked at my mama in silence, not knowing what to say. I know she sensed my uneasiness and said reassuringly, "Don't worry baby, I am ready. I have had five beautiful children. I am tired and want to go home to be with Lisa." Shortly after, my mama fell asleep and I saw it as an opportunity to go out into the hallway to try and figure out the right thing to do for her. I sat there, conflicted with the situation in front of me when, from my mama's room; there came a sound I had never heard before. My mama was screaming in pain. The nurse rushed in and told me the medication was wearing off. She said my mother's condition was worsening, but they were not authorized to give her a stronger medication to ease her pain. The nurse said only my mother's doctor could prescribe that, and he would not be back until the morning. For the next few hours, I stayed with my mom, helpless, as she alternated between passing out from the exhaustion of screaming and being jolted out a dead sleep from the pain.

By the time the morning and her doctor arrived, my decision was clear. I would consent to putting my mother into a hospice where they could make her comfortable with any and all the medication she needed to ease her suffering. There was absolutely no way I would let her go through another night like this.

I learned that night that life is not always fair. It will deal you a hand, and you either play the cards or you fold. Sometimes we will choose to bluff our way through it until we find the courage to do the right thing. My mama showed me the peace that comes with accepting life on life's terms and making the best of the hand you have. She taught me to be brave past my own fears, to serve her in the moment she needed me most. I learned that, at these defining moments, we are given the opportunity to be better than we know we can. To serve another beyond our own fears is one of the greatest reasons to be alive.

I also learned that death is not the end. My mama showed me that with her genuine desire to move past this existence. She had this knowingness that this was the next natural step in her life, and she had no fear. She knew that she would be better off than what she would leave behind.

I mean if we think about it, the body is so fragile and can die a million different ways, right? But the power of our spirit or soul is forever. Some days I swear I can still feel my sister Lisa's presence and she has been dead for more than 15 years.

When my mom finally passed, it was clear that death is not the end. It seems that once we are free of our physical body, we go to another level of consciousness. Since we no longer have a body, we no longer have the physical needs for things such as food, housing and medicine. Without having to depend on a body and the finite life expectancy that goes with it, we no longer have the fear of death. We are free to explore our unlimited potential on a new level. We could paint or garden or master an instrument for an infinite amount of time. We have no need for title, prestige or money, so we are truly free of ego and all human frailties.

With my mama's departure, I was given the honor to serve her as she crossed over. I am grateful for the gift of being able to do that for my mama and to give her comfort, dignity and peace.

TO DESERVE THE BEST

We all deserve the best that life has to offer. But to deserve the best, I have to do and be my best. Otherwise, it simply doesn't add up. For example, does it make sense to say, "I am very successful but I never work at it? I am in top physical condition but I never work out, and I eat crap?" These things don't go together, right?

Being my absolute best is self-discipline defined. It possesses me when everything else challenges me. I believe it takes the highest level of discipline to achieve my goals and dreams. It doesn't matter if I'm tired, in a bad mood, or whether it's to my liking—to be successful, doing my best is an absolute.

Consistency is also a key element to excellence. I must consistently execute at the highest level to succeed. I like to compare it to running a fine dining establishment. Let's say I go to my favorite restaurant and they make my favorite dish, just the way I like it. I go back a second time and a different chef is on duty, and he doesn't make my meal quite the same way. I may give them a third opportunity. The third time around, another chef is cooking, and doesn't make my meal right, either.

At this point, I am done with that restaurant and will never eat there again. This experience taught me that the only way to succeed in being my best is to exemplify excellence, reliably.

It's easy to be great for a day, challenging to do so for a week, but difficult to sustain greatness. To achieve this, I am a student, mastering the art of sustained passion. The foundations of this passion are *focus and discipline.*

To *focus* means to *pay attention.* I must pay attention to every aspect of my life. When I'm focused, I am more productive and efficient in every way. Passion comes easily when I'm focused on what I'm doing, such as enjoying a meal or spending time with a loved one. Focus also helps me make better choices and stay the course to success.

As stated, *discipline* is to *always do my best.* I also know that when I do my best, I feel great, and feeling great about myself is *self-esteem.* A person earns high self-esteem by never giving up, working hard and always doing their best. Those people are more goal-oriented and passionate about life.

It is only from a constant state of *focus* and *discipline* that I can master and sustain passion, live to my fill potential, and create a life worth living.

Above all, I would never presume to do this on my own. Only my ego would let me stand on my soapbox and profess that. I'm able to do, be and deserve the best life has to offer because of God's love, and the support of the people with whom I'm blessed.

I AM GRATEFUL

Gratitude is the life-skill of appreciating everything and everyone. Even the little things, such as a breath of fresh air, or a new day, are blessings. I have a morning ritual before I get out of bed where I practice an *attitude of gratitude*. As I lie there, I breathe in and say to myself, "I am breathing." This is important because if I was not breathing, I probably wouldn't have much to be grateful for, right?" Next, I breathe out and say, "I am grateful I get another day to live my best life." I then repeat this process and go through a gratitude list, which includes my family, health, career, friends, success and more.

I add to this *grateful mindset* by saying, "The grass is not greener on the other side. It is greenest where I water it." The mental picture of caring for the people, things and circumstances in my life inspires me to appreciate what I have versus what I don't.

I am even thankful for every challenge in my life because I see it as an opportunity to learn, grow and become a better person. These challenges are lessons waiting to be learned, but only if I open my mind and heart to them with a deep sense of appreciation.

I am grateful for every tear I shed because it lets me know I'm alive. I choose to smile as I walk through the rain because I know it can't rain all the time, and it will eventually give way to the light of a new day.

I choose to celebrate my victories with humility, for humility is the path to gratitude. A boastful attitude is detrimental to happiness and counter-productive to nurturing thankfulness.

I plant the seeds of gratitude everywhere I go by always saying "please" and "thank you." This gesture recognizes others for who they are and what they do.

I practice an *Attitude of Gratitude* every day. If someone asks me, "How are you doing?" I always reply, "I am grateful." Just the sound of saying it is a reminder of the life I have been blessed with.

I am a huge advocate of "paying it forward," that simple act of giving without expectation. Nothing completes me more than serving others, only because I know it is the right thing to do. *Paying it forward* is powerful and restores people's faith in one another.

I know that it is often difficult to feel grateful when I'm struggling, in pain, or have suffered a loss. At such times, my mindset doesn't promote positive thinking. Consumed by the sadness in front of me, I can often dwell in darkness and despair.

My natural path has always been focused on learning how to get through these times in a healthy manner, and become a better person. First, I need to give myself permission to experience what I am feeling. This can often get messy, and becomes easy to feel guilty and beat myself up for appearing weak.

It is at these moments, more than ever, that I need to remind myself to honor every feeling I am experiencing, at all costs. I don't pretend everything is fine when it is not. To do so would demonstrate a lack of gratitude for myself. Imperfections and all, I will always appreciate the gift that is me.

I like to keep a journal and write down everything I am feeling. The cool thing about this is that, when I am having a bad day, I can look back and see how I behaved and acted. I can see the pattern that created that bad day and left me ungrateful, while making sure not to repeat it. On a good day, I can look back at what I wrote and learn what promoted positive thinking.

Lastly, I invest in my personal relationship with a higher power. This unwavering belief has always instilled the deepest sense of gratitude in my life. It lifts me above my worst self to a better me. And for that, *I am grateful*.

THE POWER OF WORDS

Words can do great harm but they also have incredible power to heal. The admonition, "Choose your words wisely," is testament to that. Words can wound, leaving a person full of hurt and self-doubt. But, at their best, words have the strength to inspire us past our fears and insecurities.

"Stick and stones may break my bones but words will never hurt me." I'm unsure about this. It sounds reasonable, but its real-life application is lacking. Words *do* hurt and can cause serious damage.

My earliest recollection of the power of words was when my mother, who was divorced from my dad and living apart from us, would promise to come take me for a visit. My mother would say, "I'm going to come get you next Saturday, OK? I promise."

When that Saturday came, I was so excited. I was dressed and waiting on the front steps of our 15th Street flat. It was a hot summer day and I ate a Popsicle while I waited. Soon, all that was left was the wooden stick. I figured my mom would be here any minute, as promised, so I passed the time by rubbing the stick back and forth on the concrete step. I did this for what seemed like hours. I wore the stick down to a point. Still, my mother never showed.

She later apologized when we spoke on the phone and made some adult-like excuse that I did not understand. She promised it would not happen next week. The following Saturday was a repeat performance, and all I had to show for it was a worn-down Popsicle stick.

I couldn't tell you how many times this happened. I can tell you that I eventually carved a 3-inch groove in the cement step with those Popsicle sticks.

On occasion, I feel nostalgic and pass by the old flat on 15th Street. I can still see evidence of my mother's broken promises.

This taught me a hard lesson: Always be a person of my word. If I say I am going to do something, I do it. Otherwise, I am a liar and no one will trust me. More importantly, I never want to cause the kind of disappointment I experienced.

The people closest to us are the ones we abuse most with our words. Maybe it's because they are convenient or we know they have no choice because they are our family. Maybe it's because we know they love us and will ultimately forgive most things.

For this reason, we must value the gift of family by offering them the kindest words of love and understanding. We must honor them, celebrating them with accolades. Family is our most precious resource, and I thank God for helping me realize this every day.

So, what inspires people to thoughtlessly hurt one another with their words? For me, whenever I behaved less than my best, it was to make myself look better than someone, or to win another's approval. At other times, it was because I was selfish, insecure and full of ego.

I love the line from the Disney classic *Bambi* where Thumper speaks unkindly to Bambi, and the bunny's mother reminds him of his dad's rule.

"What does your father tell you?" asks Thumper's mom.

Sheepishly, Thumper responds, "If you can't say something nice, don't say anything at all."

Following this rule, though, is sometimes hard to do. It requires understanding, acceptance, compassion and restraint to choose words that heal.

Consider Martin Luther King Jr.'s "I had a dream." Or the much quoted, "Failure is not an option." These are powerful and inspiring words. Imagine if everything that came out of our mouths possessed that type of purpose and intent? Every conversation we shared would have the potential for greatness.

So, why did I choose to sit on the stairs, waiting every Saturday for a mother who never showed? Because at the end of every apologetic phone call was the sound of my mama's voice, saying, "I love you." Those are the three most powerful words, ever.

MEDITATION

I recently read the alarming statistic that about 70 percent of most people's thoughts are negative. And about 90 percent of people suffer from some form of depression. This is an epidemic, and a battle within that must be fought on a personal level.

I strive to manage my negative thinking through exercise, proper nutrition, supplementation (vitamins and Chinese herbs), good sleeping habits and meditation. I have found great success. My life is better because I live by a positive mindset. It is difficult at times, but well worth the effort and benefits.

Some days when I am feeling negative, I look in the mirror and chant the mantra with a forced smile on my face, "Feeling good and getting better." I repeat it until my mood shifts, my smile is genuine, and I am back in a positive space.

It is important to acknowledge and honor all our feelings...to embrace them and feel everything. This is who we are, *feeling* beings. We should never ignore our emotions. My mantra—*feeling good and getting better*— is a great way to climb out of that dark place.

I've proven that as long as I never give up, and always do my best, positive thoughts can overcome.

The answers we seek are inside. We must turn inward to find the truth. Meditation is one of the important steps. There is no right or wrong behavior in meditation. It is simply "me time." We all deserve this kind of personal attention. Meditation is a self-care activity where we're encouraged to love ourselves. The peace and joy felt by those who meditate enters the world as positive energy. Here are some universal steps that help facilitate effective meditation:

- Find your posture (a comfortable but aware position).
- Close your eyes.
- Be mindful of your breath.
- Focus on the nothingness that you see.
- Clear your mind of all clutter and negativity.
- Think as you breathe in, "I am breathing."
- Think as you breathe out, "I am grateful."

The practical effort to focus on our breathing cuts through the *mind clutter* that constantly tries to invade our thinking and keep us agitated. With repeated effort, we can reach the goal of calming our mind until it's clear of thoughts. As we practice, we see that the process of meditation takes on its own energy. The result is peace, serenity and a calmness that opens us to new insights.

Meditative reflections
Are the center
Of pure thought.
See this energy
And find the focus
That will lead
You to balance.
It is at this
Point of being
That we begin
To discover
The meaning
Of truth
And not the self-willed
Perception of
What we believe
It to be.

CENTER MYSELF

I visualize a circle. Every point on the circumference of that circle is equidistant from the center. When I am centered, I see everything and everyone with a sense of equanimity. It offers me balance and serenity. Centering myself keeps me even keeled through life's ups and downs.

I visualize an image of the scale of Lady Justice. I see myself running from one end of that scale to the other, trying to center myself. This is how life is for me when I'm unbalanced. I expend so much wasted energy going back and forth. Like a ship trying to right itself in a storm, my sole purpose becomes consumed in steadying my boat. It is near impossible to move forward and progress in life when I am in this unstable state.

When I am unbalanced, I am stressed, depressed and desperate. I make bad choices and never seem to do the right thing. I dig a deep hole with edges that are hard to climb.

I am devoted to centering myself. To create this balance, it's important to feed my mind, body and spirit equally. When all three elements of myself are nourished, I am at my best. When I neglect any one of these, the imbalance makes everything more difficult.

Centering helps me flow like water. Optimal balance of *mind, body* and spirit gives me the ability to be fluid—like water moving down a river. Water does not go through the rocks; it flows over, under and around. The flowing water intuitively adjusts, gaining momentum in the process. This is where I think the term "going with the flow" originates. When I am fluid, life feels effortless. I become the definition of balance and maintain a state of equilibrium.

I also view balance like the three legs that support a stool. If any of those legs—my mind, body or spirit— are weak, the stool tips from the stress.

It is easy to be great when things are going my way, but can I be great when life is difficult? Maintaining balance through my shortcomings and sufferings builds character, and makes me a better person.

Eat enough. Sleep enough. Play enough. Work enough. Reflect enough. And most of all, love enough. I live from love because love creates optimal balance. It helps me to live my best life.

Balance is nurtured through the understanding that love is all-inclusive. I honor every emotion that makes us human by processing it through the filter of love. It gives me the strength to forgive, understand and accept life on life's terms.

Call me a lost romantic, but I honestly believe love conquers all. Love gives me the hope to be resilient in the face of adversity and pain. Love gives me the tools to negotiate time and space with a true sense of balance. I make better choices and take the right actions.

The pursuit of balance is often the most overlooked aspect of our lives. We get so caught in doing, and "keeping up with the Joneses," we forget that our greatest purpose in life is to LOVE.

Love begins by loving myself. I am no good to anyone unless I am good to myself. I am my own best investment, so I am committed to centering myself. A few things that help me cultivate life-balance are to spend time alone every day, share quality time with my family and friends, take time out to do nothing, humbly accept my limitations, recognize that I don't do this thing called "life" alone, learn to say "No" sometimes, and know when to let go. The last one, letting go, has been my greatest teacher in centering myself.

From the center,
Every point is
Equidistant.
So, if we are
Centered,
Everything
Will be equal,
Without judgment
Or odds to
Set us apart.

10 POUNDS

From as early as age 10, my weight was a huge factor in achieving goals and getting approval. I was actively competing in martial arts tournaments and making weight was constantly an issue. I was a short and stocky kid by stature and losing 10 pounds was always on my agenda.

At about the same time, I started doing some local commercials and television shows. It was drilled into my head by casting agents that the camera adds 10 pounds, so I was always on a mission to lose weight, even when I did not need to.

I would spend days training in a silver plastic sweat suit to drop 10 pounds. I would sit at the table, looking at my food like it was the enemy. Anything I ate became a source of guilt. I was like an alcoholic, where one drink is too many and a thousand, never enough. If I ate chocolate chip cookies, I could never eat just one. I had to eat the whole bag, and hated myself after.

The other battle I had with food, which created guilt and caused me to overeat at times, developed from having grown up poor. I was always expected to eat everything that was put on my plate at dinner. If I didn't, I was made to stand in the hallway, holding my plate of uneaten food. If I did not eat my food that night, I could expect it at breakfast the next morning.

My love/hate relationship with food took its toll on me mentally, and fed my low self-worth. The food that satisfied my appetite the most was the praise and approval I earned when I made weight for a competition, or when someone complimented me on how thin I looked in a picture.

This behavior dominated most of my life as I continued in martial arts and, eventually, in a music career. When I first signed on with a talent manager, he asked me if I would be willing to lose weight. Even as an adult, those 10 pounds haunted me. It seemed that being accepted and reaching the success I desired depended on losing those 10 pounds.

Today, I still believe I could always lose 10 pounds, but I am kinder and gentler with myself in the process. I accept God made me as he intended. I embrace my short stockiness in all its glory.

I now practice a healthy outlook on eating and exercising. I have thrown out my men's fitness magazines and the aspiration for six-pack abs. Even on the craziest of days, I find a way to exercise. I embrace a philosophy that a little bit of something is better than a whole lot of nothing. I take the stairs instead of the elevator. I will intentionally park farther away from the mall entrance and walk. I make it a habit to do pushups and sit-ups during the commercial breaks of my favorite television program. I love to walk around my business when I'm on a conference call.

I don't always like to exercise, though. To overcome my resistance, I have to tell myself that I deserve the best in life, and that includes optimal health. Anytime I find myself not wanting to work out, this is the reason I make sure I do. I understand if I go any amount of time without "watering my grass," I could find myself eating that whole bag of chocolate chip cookies.

I now look at a healthy lifestyle as a method of self-love. I find myself taking the time to listen to my breath and just know that I am alive. I am thankful for my health. I demonstrate that appreciation for my body by practicing martial arts, riding my bike, hitting the gym and eating right most days.

Whenever I exercise consistently, I am full of energy and feel more passionate about living life. I also dig the confidence that comes from being able to fit into my favorite jeans.

BE CONTENT, BUT NEVER SATISFIED

While it's important to be content with where you are today, always strive to be and do better. Successful people don't focus on what they've done. They focus on what they have to do. Live in the present. Remember, the *present* is called *the present* because it's a gift. Be fully present with every person you interact with, every day.

Use what you've learned in the past to help you live better today. Focus on being the best person possible. What matters most is what you contribute to society, your family and yourself today.

Make it a priority to seek out and develop quality relationships. From your employees to your mentors and friends, spend your time with quality people.

Define what "quality" means to you. They should exemplify all the qualities you admire and aspire to be. They should inspire you to greatness. They should offer you constructive criticism that helps you recognize your unlimited potential.

The people in your life should be one of your greatest reasons to love and do what you do.

CAN YOU BE GREAT WHEN LIFE IS HARD?

We live in a world of immediate gratification. Our children have been conditioned to believe that they should get what they want, when they want it. This sense of entitlement makes it convenient for them to give up and quit when something is hard or not to their liking. Again, *it's easy to be great when things are going your way.* But can you be great when things aren't going your way?

Nothing grows in complacency and comfort. It might appear safe but eventually gives way to routine and boredom. You may find yourself waking up 20 or 50 years from now with a gold watch and a pension, asking yourself, "What the hell happened to my life?"

Life is messy. As I've said before, I do some of my best learning lying flat on my face. Adversity holds the greatest opportunities to build our character and self-esteem—if we don't give up. Hard work is the key to success and living the best quality life possible. If we are willing to give 100 percent and not give up, even when it's tough, we can achieve anything. Commit. Persevere. Each challenge is an opportunity to be better.

You've got to have faith.
It's hope without fear.
The knowing that a happy ending
Is just around the corner.
That at the end of a rainbow
Is more than just a pot of gold,
It's the beginning of
All the endless possibilities
If you would just have the faith
To believe when there is
Nothing left to believe in,
To hold on when all
You want to do is to just let go.
Faith challenges you to give more
When you feel like you have so little.
Faith is love beyond fear,
A moment in present time
Where you honestly believe
With a child's smile
That peace is the path
You deserve to walk.

MAKE THAT CHANGE!

Why is it that with all the available information on how to achieve success and happiness, some choose to improve the quality of their lives, while others choose not to? Even though we all have access to the same information and tools, why is it that some succeed while others fail?

The key to making real change is to recognize our most treasured values. For example, values such as integrity, respect, and tolerance may be core values that we would not give up for all the money in the world. Once we have clearly defined our values, we can begin to recognize our true purpose in life. Why are we here? What impact and difference will we make to this world? At the end of our lives, what do we want to be remembered for? What legacy will we leave behind?

Next, we need to recognize the difference between our self-will and our bigger purpose to serve the world. The lines here are often blurred because self-will can trick us into believing that serving our needs is justified, even honorable. You've heard the term, "Service Above Self?" There is nothing more gratifying than to give to and do for others. Perhaps you've heard that "you can only keep what you have by giving it away." Selfish people who hoard and squander their wealth often end up unhappy and living empty and unfulfilled lives. Acting from the fear-based thinking—*I will never have enough* thinking—will always deplete our soul.

See the baby
Take his first step.
So much thought
And preparation
Are involved.
The importance,
Negotiation and planning
Bear great significance.
The child is amazed,
Overwhelmed, excited,
Delighted and determined
To complete his task.
He lifts his appendage
With calculated precision
And gingerly, no...*awkwardly*,
Leans forward
To plant it firmly in
Front of himself.
The red alert is over
And the green light
Signals a successful mission.
The first step has been
Taken and many more
Trips lie in the future.
Just imagine what
It's gonna be like
When he starts running.

A LEAP OF FAITH

As we climbed to 10,000 feet in a rickety Cessna, I sat among three experienced sky divers and a well-seasoned pilot. They projected an energy of deep respect and awareness for what we were about to experience.

One skydiver, who had 260 jumps under his belt—all in the past six months—was totally serene. I watched his calm eyes as he peered out the window to take in the morning sky.

I captured the Zen that filled the experienced jumper's eyes to steady my breath. I closed my eyes and meditated. I felt no fear in this tiny cockpit, only a deep sense of humility for what was about to take place. As we reached the proper altitude to make our jump, the paper-thin side hatch opened. I looked out and witnessed God's earth as I'd never seen it. As I stepped out onto the wing, my meditative breath gave way to the deafening power of the wind. My tandem instructor, strapped to my back, shouted in my ear, "Get ready!" I stepped off the wing and took the "leap of faith" that sent me hurtling toward earth at 120 miles per hour!

The incredible rush clarified what I witnessed in the eyes of those skydivers. Now, it was alive in *my* heart. As I fell to the earth, I peeled off all layers of complacency and ego. I felt the truth of God's love, knowing I was not going to die, but live life in a way I had never experienced. It was euphoric in every sense, dancing in heaven.

The instructor put his gloved hand on my forehead, and pulled my head against his chest, a position we rehearsed. This was the signal to brace for the parachute's opening. As our chute was deployed, the sensation brought me to a new level of consciousness.

Everything went silent and slowed, almost to a standstill. I adjusted my goggles and focused my eyes on the fantastic view below me. I had never seen this great and beautiful world from this vantage point or in such a way. At that moment, I felt my joy give way to a sense of sadness. How could any of us believe we are any more significant than beautiful, powerful Mother Earth?

We are often selfish, repeatedly harming her for convenience, "progress," and profit. It made me ashamed to be part of humankind. But as she reached for me with her arms stretched out, I felt forgiven.

Each breath I took was timeless. I was present in each moment, feeling the simple joy of being. I understood God gives us these moments to know the power of His love. My skydiving adventure was so much more than jumping out of an airplane. It was truly a *Leap of Faith*.

IT'S A NEW DAY

Today is a new day—a chance to start all over...a clean slate...a blank canvas. We can close the door on yesterday and open a new one with the anticipation of a child on Christmas morning. We shouldn't look back at the closed door with regret. It is only by looking ahead that we can see the opportunity and hope that awaits us.

We can build upon the confidence earned from every lesson learned on the path to today. We are not defined by past mistakes. They are simply lessons waiting to be learned. They can only define us today if we keep making the same mistakes.

Dream big or don't bother. Commit to the pursuit of excellence and never settle for "I tried." Because once we have tasted greatness—through hard work, doing our best and never giving up—we will never be OK with "OK" again. You feel me?

Time is worth more than money. We must not squander it just to add a few more zeros to our bank accounts. We can always make more money, but we can't make more time once we have lost it. Spend time with those we love, and it enriches our lives more than anything.

We can dedicate ourselves to the pursuit of life balance. Let's manage stress more gracefully, through humility and acceptance. With sustained passion, continued learning and constant effort, we will succeed.

Children are our greatest teachers. We mustn't ever find ourselves saying, "Children say the darnedest things." To say so would diminish the truth children speak. Childlike innocence makes some adults uncomfortable because it's so honest. We should actively listen to children because they speak the most truth. Their ability to live in the moment is the best model for how we can be our true self.

How important it is to take time in each new day to reflect, turn inward and embrace the silence? Everything we need to know is inside us, and has been since birth. We are the architects of our lives. Who better to design it than us?

LOVE IS ALL THAT REALLY MATTERS

When we choose to live from an open heart of love, we give ourselves the opportunity to learn, grow and live better. Living from a closed heart, based on fear, takes more energy and attention, leaving us paralyzed and unable to grow.

It takes courage to change. We have to take that first step if we're going to go anywhere. The great thing is that we are not always going to succeed, so we'll get plenty of practice to be resilient and act out of love. Keep on. When we falter, it feels much better to feel love than it does to be afraid. Let's live in love in every aspect of our lives, and watch the miracles unfold. We are the great mystery, and being present in every moment of the life we are blessed with helps tell our story. Remember, it takes great courage to love. Loving challenges us to be vulnerable, and lead with an open heart. With practice, living from an open heart becomes as natural as breathing.

Love is all that matters. In the end, love is the greatest reason for our being. We live for it, long for it and thrive in it.

Love is not a greeting card. It's all-inclusive, warts and all. Sometimes love is pure joy and bliss. At other moments, love is as haunting and melancholy as a Billie Holiday song. Love pulls back our covers and leaves us vulnerable. It challenges us to give more than we ever thought possible.

I choose to live and breathe and move in love and all it offers. On the best days, love fills every part of my being. On my worst days, love provides shelter. Love is truly the greatest gift we are given.

Alive!
What is inside your heart?
Choose to tear down
The thick, high walls
That keeps out all the light
And make you feel nothing
Except the monotony
Of making the same mistake
Over and over and over,
While asking yourself, "Why?"
I challenge you
To laugh 10 times a day and
To always be in love
With yourself and others,
And with life in all its
Glorious mysteries and
Funky twists and turns.
Find those places in you
Where no amount of
Distractions or lies
Can prevent you from
Hearing the truth that
Cries out from your soul.
"I'm alive in here.
I am alive!"
And then all you'll hear is
The sound of silence.
You've broken through
To the other side,

Past your fears,
Past your past,
Into the gap of unlimited
Potential, where
Love is the light
That shines through the
Darkness in your heart.
I am humbled
To share my heart with you
And will always choose
To love completely
Each and every time
God grants me this opportunity.
This love is God's gift that asks us
To fully appreciated it
In all its simplicity.

HAPPY ON PURPOSE

Happiness is a choice, and I choose to make it my purpose to learn, practice and master. Do I have to work at it some days? Absolutely. Am I always happy? No. But I view being happy like any relationship I choose. I take the good with the bad, because I am in love with happiness.

My life was not always sunshine and flowers. My earliest childhood memories were of living in a foster home. After that, an abusive single parent raised my sisters and me, and, at times, we were on welfare and food stamps. I grew up in a tough neighborhood, where drugs, gangs and violence were part of everyday life. From the circumstances of my upbringing, I grew up conditioned to believe that being unhappy was normal. I romanticized it like a starving musician who suffers for his art. One of my favorite songs as a young adult that summed up my thinking was, "Glad To Be Unhappy," by the jazz singer Billie Holiday. I wore being unhappy like a badge of honor, and as an excuse for all my shortcomings and failures.

Sadness had been as close as my next of kin. No matter how many times happiness came my way, I somehow closed the door, conditioned to be unhappy.

As the saying goes, "You don't know what you don't know." But even then, I knew something wasn't right. I can recall standing on a stage, singing to thousands of people, but feeling alone and unhappy. No matter my level of success, I always felt a deep sense of despair and unworthiness.

Gratefully, I have been saved many times by God's love and mercy. I have been blessed with little miracles, disguised as life lessons. I've shared many of them in this book, but none of them alone was a defining moment. God does everything in his time, so I guess he was just working on me at His own pace. I also believe God helps those who help themselves. I know I've got to do the hard work.

I asked myself, "If happiness is a choice, then what choices do I need to make?" First, I must learn to be happy with me. I've got to accept myself for who I am, imperfections and all. That begins by letting go of past mistakes. I choose to acknowledge them as life lessons, teaching me to be a better person. I figure if I can be OK with me, I can be OK with others, and life.

A big part of choosing to be happy is being grateful. I practice an *Attitude of Gratitude* every day. If someone asks me, "How're you doing?" I always reply, "I am grateful." Saying this reminds me to appreciate everything and everyone.

I find an important part of choosing to be happy is having what is called a "white belt mindset." I stand by the philosophy that I'm "always a student and never a master." There's always something to learn, right? Someone who is learning is happier than someone who believes they know it all.

The greatest gift that choosing to be happy offers me is that it teaches me to live in the moment. I've read that if you live in the past, you are depressed; if you project into the future, you are anxious; but if you are in the moment, you are at peace. Yesterday is but a memory and tomorrow is a dream. But If I can be right here, right now, I can appreciate and embrace every second the present has to offer.

I also found happiness when I discovered what my purpose is in this world. We are all unique and incredibly special. We have a purpose beyond our own selfish needs. When I came to understand that my purpose in life was to serve others, happiness came easily. Serving others always puts a big smile on my face. Whether I am speaking at the county jail, working with battered women in a half-way house, or teaching martial arts to a child with special needs, I find great joy and humility in giving back. I feel the most at peace when I serve and "pay it forward."

The choice to be happy gives me the courage to be vulnerable, live from an open heart, and to love completely. No matter how painful that is at times, it is worth every bit of suffering I have and will endure. Love is the purpose of my happiness.

ABOUT THE AUTHOR

PHOTO: J. Michael Tucker

BRANNON BELISO is a giver who believes in paying it forward. His passion is to serve and create with relevancy. He lives in the present with a sense of purpose, to make a difference and impact lives.

Brannon has lived many lifetimes in one. He is a published author, speaker and mentor. He's had a career as a disc jockey, sang to tens of thousands of people, competed in and won more than 100 open martial arts tournaments, was in the delivery room at age 16 watching his first son be born, has jumped out of an airplane, serenaded the president of the Philippines, and married his one true love.

Brannon's belief is that we all deserve the best life has to offer, if we choose to do and be our best. You will hear him say, "If I'm not getting better, I'm getting worse—and *better* is what I'm all about." Brannon constantly strives to be a better version of himself through dedicated learning.

Brannon lives to love, and that love is the light that guides him past his fears, onto the path of happiness. Love is all that matters because without it, nothing in life has much value. Living from a humble heart, he wakes up every morning, grateful that he gets another day to live his best life.

Brannon writes because he believes we all have a story that deserves to be told. He chose to share his story with you in the hope that it will inspire you to live, learn and grow.

For more information on Brannon Beliso's talks, workshops, and coaching, please email him: professor@onemartialarts.com.

RECOMMENDED READING

The Miracle of Mindfulness by Thich Nhat Hanh
The Four Agreements by Don Miguel Ruiz
Good to Great by Jim Collins
The Happiness Advantage by Shawn Achor
The Tao of Jeet Kune Do by Bruce Lee
Delivering Happiness by Tony Hsieh
Way of the Peaceful Warrior by Dan Millman
Mindset by Carol Dweck
The Dark Side of the Light Chasers by Debbie Ford
The Tao of Pooh by Benjamin Hoff
Tribes: We Need You to Lead Us by Seth Godin
The Prophet by Kahlil Gibran
The Artist's Way: A Spiritual Path to Higher Creativity by Julia Cameron

CPSIA information can be obtained
at www.ICGtesting.com
Printed in the USA
JSHW010328050523
41190JS00001B/9